The Tao
of the
Jump Shot

The Tao
of the
Jump Shot

AN EASTERN APPROACH TO LIFE AND BASKETBALL

John Fitzsimmons Mahoney

Introduction by Bill Walton

Seastone
BERKELEY, CALIFORNIA

Published by: Seastone, an imprint of Ulysses Press
                 P.O. Box 3440
                 Berkeley, CA 94703-3440

                    Library of Congress Cataloging-in-Publication Data
Mahoney, John Fitzsimmons.
     The Tao of the jump shot : an eastern approach to life and basketball /
  John Fitzsimmons Mahoney ; introduction by Bill Walton.
       p.   cm.
     Includes bibliographical references and index.
     ISBN 1-56975-186-2 (alk. paper)
     1. Basketball—Psychological aspects.   2. Basketball—Offense.
  3. Taoism.   I. Title.
  GV889.2.M34   1999   99-24740
  796.323'01—dc21   CIP

Printed in the USA by R. R. Donnelley & Sons

10 9 8 7 6 5 4 3 2 1

Editor: Steven Zah Schwartz
Production staff: Lily Chou, David Wells
Design: Leslie Henriques, Sara Glaser

Distributed in the United States by Publishers Group West, in Canada by Raincoast Books, and in Great Britain and Europe by Airlift Book Company

Illustrations: Zen calligraphy by Eun (1598-1679), *p. 104*; Sengai (1750-1837), *p. 27*; Ryokau (1758-1831), *p. 16*; Tesshu (1836-1888), *p. 61*; Takuro Kazushi, *pp. 10, 74*. Basketball figures by Doug McCarthy, *p. 20*.

To my wife Anna
singer, dancer, actress and perfect soul mate

TABLE OF CONTENTS

ACKNOWLEDGEMENTS

I would like to thank my friend Jerry Anderson for his perceptive and knowledgeable comments on the text.

Introduction
by Bill Walton

In *The Tao of the Jump Shot*, John Mahoney has captured the philosophical, metaphysical, historical, cultural, and societal importance of the ultimate weapon in the perfect game.

Basketball has always been my life, the game my religion, the gym my church. Everything that goes on in the game corresponds to life's daily battles. For me the most interesting parts of the game have always been the mental aspects: the preparation, dreams, visions, goals, the challenges of having to be the best in a confined area with nine other supremely conditioned and skilled athletes all striving to be the king. The ultimate winners eventually reach their peak because of their unstoppable ability to quickly outthink their opponents and anticipate the next play before anyone else does.

The Tao of the Jump Shot is a fascinating explanation of the historical importance and relationship of the game of basketball to this eternal struggle. The book is laid out magnificently, as if it were a game—broken into two halves, with introductions, warm-ups, and the finest points intimately dissected in a very readable way, explaining the mechanics, the thought processes, the development, the balance—all the elements that go into an exceptional event. This book flows like a beautiful game, filled with human drama, suspense and uncertainty, played by the game's greatest players. It brings together the interlocking foundations of the most diverse disciplines—physics, mathematics, history, geography and religion—and shows how the human being forms the bridge between them all.

As the book builds, chapter by chapter, with vignettes on the pieces that create the ultimate puzzle of the game, one is exhilarated by the building of pressure—by the sense that you are in the game, that you are the game, and that the ball is now an extension of your mind. Reading *The Tao of the Jump Shot* lets you become the artist, makes you the creator, the one dictating the tempo.

You become a good basketball player by breaking the game down and working on the individual parts. The sum of those parts is where the dream of perfection connects with physical reality. You work on each individual skill separately, examine each stage of physical motion. That's what John Mahoney has done with all of his chapters, taking all the little pieces and dissecting them, showing us what they are and how to execute each movement. He relates each piece to history and religion, to all the different elements that go into making up the whole.

Obviously John Mahoney has a terrific jump shot. Clearly he has spent a lifetime dreaming—his brilliance truly emanates from these dreams in the way he is able to break down the nuances of body movement, spatial relationships and hand-eye co-ordination and put all of these in the context of the totality of the universe in a truly inspiring fashion. I have never been able to separate basketball from life, and to see it all come together into such a pleasurable, compact, concise read is sheer joy. This is a book that encapsulates the essence of the world for people who live the game of basketball.

But this book is not just for players: It's for anyone who wants to understand the game. In basketball the jump shot is the peak, the thing that sets you apart. The ability to get that ball and make a shot in somebody else's face—that is the ultimate weapon. A casual observer might say, "That's really easy—the players are smooth and fluid," without realizing how that fluidity, smoothness and gracefulness come from a lifetime of passion, a lifetime of incredibly hard work, discipline, organization, sacrifice and commitment—all the things that go into making you good at whatever it is you do. This book reaches far beyond basketball.

Basketball is the perfect game because you can create the battle in your mind. This book expands your mind. It gives you clarity. It gives you direction. It gives you new horizons that will help you understand what it is you're doing and where it all fits in our world. Someone who reads this book who isn't into basketball will learn how to take something apart, study the pieces and see how it fits back together with everything else. You can plug in whatever you do in place of the jump shot.

That's what my great coaches (six of whom are in the Basketball Hall of Fame) did: they didn't coach basketball *per se*. They were teachers, and not so much of basketball, but of life. They taught values; they taught things that would help develop our character and make us better people, knowing that ultimately we wouldn't be able to play basketball anymore, that our bodies would someday break down. But once we had the foundation and the format, once we had the ability to learn—the knowledge to build a life, to build a game—then we would be able to go on and do whatever it was we'd choose to do.

To appreciate this book, to enjoy and respect it, you don't need a foundation in Eastern religion and philosophy. The way John Mahoney presents *The Tao of the Jump Shot*, it's all about the flow, the natural progression that comes to you when you are in the zone. One of the great things my teachers gave me in basketball was the ability to create the zone—to not wait for the zone to come my way through happenstance or luck. We are responsible for creating the factors that allow us to be in the zone on command. That's what a lot of the Eastern metaphysical disciplines are all about—finding that perfect state, finding that sense of eternal sunshine, and not just finding it but being able to create and sustain it. When you reach that level, the world and the game are yours, and there's nothing a bigger, stronger, rougher, faster opponent can do to take it away. This book, like the game of basketball, is about finding that perfect rhythm, that flow of the river, of the sun bursting through the clouds and continuing on its perfect arc, like the arc of the jump shot.

These thoughts and dreams are what have shaped my life in basketball. *The Tao of the Jump Shot* takes it all to a new level. The factors John Mahoney brings together from all the different disciplines have certainly sparked a renewed interest, a renewed love for the game itself. But beyond that they challenge me to take my life and game to new heights. And those new heights can only be reached by the ever-inquisitive mind, always asking why? what? where? and when?

As I read this book, it is as if I am back in Pauley Pavilion at UCLA with John Wooden, in the Portland Memorial Coliseum with Jack Ramsey and the Trailblazers, in the Boston Garden with Red Auerbach and Larry Bird, with everything crystalizing—everything coming into focus. It is as if I am in every game I have played, in every practice session I've sweated through, in every workout I've used to get ready for the ultimate battle. As this book comes to an end, everything is in perfect focus and I'm in the zone once again. The game, the ball, are in my hand and everyone else moves in slow motion as if frozen in time.

Enjoy this book. Learn to live the game of basketball — the game of life — because in the end it's all the same. Good luck, and may all your jumpers go down.

FIRST HALF

1

The Way of the Shot

ANY PHYSICAL OR MENTAL ACTIVITY that's constructive and creative and aims for perfection helps in our quest for the spiritual foundations of existence. The philosophies and metaphysics of Taoism and Zen penetrate nearly every art and every conceivable human action. They aim to infuse life with the fundamental principles of their teaching and transform the world in the process.

Eastern traditions bring us not only a religious philosophy but a teaching whose sole purpose is the awakening of humanity — to induce a living insight that transforms our relationship with reality. This radical change of state within the human being has informed all the arts, sciences, even sports. The Japanese words for archery (*kyu-∂o*), wrestling (*ju-∂o*) and swordsmanship (*ken-∂o*) all contain the ideogram *∂o* which is equivalent to the Chinese term Tao. Opening inwardly by letting go of the self allows the artist or athlete to bring the spontaneous dimension of the Way, the actionless action of the Tao, into the discipline. Unfor-

DO: the Way

tunately, modern sports inhibit this capacity, and our culture starves for the heroic dimension that's always open to us through mastery of any skill.

Although swordsmanship and martial arts appear to conflict with the ethic of non-violence, they paradoxically provide the most dramatic examples of the transformative power of Taoist and Zen teachings. Ordinary people who have come into contact with these philosophies while practicing such deadly arts have led lives of spiritual depth *and* heroic proportion. Look at the spiritual attitude of the samurai: he awakens in our minds courage and an indomitable fighting spirit combined with the most extraordinary integrity, righteousness and compassion. His artistic expression and aesthetic sensitivity are second to none. Zen is sometimes called "the religion of the samurai."

The great truth and extensive reach of Taoism and Zen become especially evident when their principles not only affect the hearts and minds of the participants but actually lead to perfecting skills. Placing the jump shot in the context of these universal teachings reveals that the mastery of any skill—physical, intellectual or artistic—can open the door to the depths of spiritual insight.

On the surface, shooting a jump shot seems a pedestrian activity, not well suited to illustrate a metaphysical doctrine such as Taoism. But looking closer at its proper execution, in isolation and under game conditions, reveals a physical and mental feat of extraordinary complexity. When the insights of Taoism and Zen shine on the mind-body coordination needed for a jump shot, new possibilities open for perfecting the shot and the spiritual awareness of the athlete. The kinetic aspect of shooting is balanced by immovable spiritual insight; physical energy integrates with mindfulness, transforming both the game and the player.

The inner dimensions of a jump shot arise because it's an alchemical mixture of power, muscle strength, coordination, balance, flexibility, finesse, explosiveness, timing and mental awareness. Its execution is the most difficult in all of sports. It involves nearly all of the more than six hundred muscle systems in the body. The difficulty of its accomplishment increases exponentially under game conditions. The shot can be taken from a standstill, off a pass, off a dribble from either hand at angles to the basket varying from zero to three hundred and sixty degrees, off a dribbling spin move or a spin from a standstill, and off a variety of fakes. It can be taken either fading away from the basket or leaning toward the basket. These conditions or movements often occur in sequential combinations, as when the athlete spins and fades during the shot's execution.

Mastery of the jump shot provides an ideal subject for exploring universal spiritual principles. It shows how developing a complex physical skill can develop the whole person. We can see its significance negatively as well: insufficient mastery of the jump shot is a major cause of poor shooting in the National Basketball Association, in college and in high school. The statistics and commentary by coaches and other experts indicate that today's player with few exceptions has not mastered the art and science of shooting a basketball. At the same time we witness greater incidence of aggression, self-inflation and other anti-social behavior.

What makes the situation particularly ironic is that the key to the perfect jump shot is effortlessness, both in its physical execution and in the mental state of the shooter. This may sound strange, since it takes years of practice to master the form, timing and biomechanics of the shot, but it won't seem strange to those familiar with the principles of Eastern teachings. In those traditions it's always a question of spontaneity, effortlessness and the controlled accident.

The game of basketball is just over a hundred years old, and the jump shot is probably only about sixty years old. The origins of the jump shot are shrouded in mystery since no one knows who first shot it. Despite this relative infancy, insight into the many dimensions of the jump shot can only enhance one's skill as a player, deepen self-understanding and increase awareness of the spiritual dimensions of existence.

In the Taoist- and Zen-inspired arts, the chief obstacle to perfection in the art and spiritual life is precisely the cognitive function of the mind. The thickest barrier between our present limited state and the dimension of true insight that's always available is the idea that we're separate islands of consciousness. Whether one is wielding a sword, shooting an arrow or shooting a basketball, the secret of perfection is to let events take their course without the thinker and thought intervening. As the Bible tells us: "It does not belong to man who is walking to direct his step."

2

Perfection

OUR IDEAS ABOUT PERFECTION ARE FUNDAMENTAL to our way of thinking and feeling. Western religious traditions tell us we lost our perfection at the Fall and are pilgrims constantly seeking to regain paradise. Despite the adage that "nothing is perfect in this world," we all have this nostalgia for perfection; it shapes our outlook on life. The dimmer the sense of lost perfection or the weaker the quest for its blessings, the stronger the grip of a limited, purely materialistic outlook.

We tend to judge the world as perfect or imperfect according to an unchangeable absolute standard. Although on the surface it looks like we're giving only a relative value to the things and events we experience, a deeper awareness of our dissatisfaction—of the partial and transitory nature of the joys we grow weary of—reveals that we judge our experience on a scale of absolute value.

As a society, we easily accept the idea of perfection and seek it as an antidote to ever-creeping mediocrity. In science and philosophy, there are those who see the universe, including the human being, as closed and self-contained. They view all things from the vantage point of a limited "I-subject," denying the inward magnetism of divine perfection, and limit intelligence to the workings of discursive thought.

Dante got to the heart of the problem in his *Inferno*, in which the damned have lost the gift of universal intellect, the inward unity that joins the human to the universe and the universe to the divine. The idea of a self-contained universe mistakes the relative for the absolute and falls well short of the idea that the human, as the synthesis of all creation, is the only being that provides an opening through which the absolute becomes conscious of itself.

Why do we have this absolute idea of perfection? It is a ray of our divine nature refracted within our consciousness. In the typical egotistical state, one's consiousness as an "I-subject" sees itself as absolutely separate from all that exists—including the body, its substantial support. Sensing that we lack something, we turn to the world and search for the key. Hungering for experience and success, we hope to fill the void with transitory pleasures. This misplaced yearning leads to doubt, conflict and excessive cerebration, all of which obscure the spiritual nature of existence and can lead to the empty stimulations of modern life.

Since it's so hard to accept our existence as it is, we develop socially respectable ways of compensating. But these are just as partial and transitory as the more debilitating escapes. Our nostalgia can't satisfactorily resolve our thirst for the unattainable perfection. Instead, our mundane solutions trap us more deeply in bleak hopelessness.

The need to judge the world as perfect or imperfect stems from the deep sense that we are exiled from paradise, a paradise we long to return to. Because I am divided within myself I sense that I am separated from the full consciousness of my being. This cuts me off from direct experience of the world and increases my yearning for an unattainable perfection, awareness of which will deliver me from my inner malaise and transform my nostalgia into a living presence of the divine.

Taoism and Zen tell us we're perfect just as we are. Our problems arise simply because we're looking in the wrong direction and need to learn a new way of seeing. Since the universe itself—including the human realm—is a harmonious balance between the forces of construction and destruction, between the good/beautiful/true and the evil/ugly/false, seeking perfection in the phenomenal world is unrealistic at best.

The universe as a dualism or harmony of opposites is powerfully symbolized by the yin-yang icon, a circle in which a white area and a black area meet in an inscribed S. The white area contains a small black circle and the black area contains a small white circle. The outside circle represents the Tao, or metaphysical unity. The black section is yin, the white section is yang: these two are the great cosmic forces whose unceasing complementarity creates the universe of "the ten thousand things." Yin is feminine, passive, receptive, negative (in the sense of electrical polarity); yang is masculine, active, expressive, positive.

The central tenet of Taoism describes the Perfect Man, the realized human who forms the bridge between the poles of these complementary pairs—between heaven, the active perfection, and earth, the passive perfection. Active perfection is comparable to the action of a potter and passive perfection to the clay. Just as the potter creates objects of many different forms from the substance of clay, so heaven and earth together produce "the ten thousand things."

Earth as pure receptivity and heaven as pure action are not visible to the senses. We can see only the forms and colors of manifested things that are produced by the sacred marriage of this primordial pair.

Buddhi, spirit or intellect, is the first-born of this union of two perfections, making humans the summit of creation. Reason emanates from intellect as the lesser from the greater. This for-

heaven and earth

gotten or ignored relationship blinds us to the non-formal dimension of intelligence; consequently, we are orphans of both heaven and earth, our metaphysical parents.

The perfect human is an exact copy of what is called the Way in Taoism, precisely because this is the one who realizes fully what Jesus said about the kingdom of heaven: It is "within you." Only the ignorant living with the notion of heaven as an afterlife turn their backs on the fullness of spirit, intellect or emptiness. To be in accord with the Way does not mean one follows a set of principles or rules. On the contrary, it means you are in accord with non-doing, which is the negation of all I-centered intention and its related thought process.

Mind, when seen as the fundamental unconscious, implies a pure action that can be described as "being so of itself." This unconscious wisdom is exemplified by the common honeybee, which produces honey and, completely on its own, the hexagonal cells of the honeycomb—a geometric arrangement that incredibly maximizes the number of cells that can be fitted into the available space. No other shape would satisfy this condition. The bee extracts and transforms the plant's nectar—the by-product of the flower's love life—into the wondrous cells of the honeycomb.

A similar act of transformative love describes the inward, creative and unconscious activity of the "perfect human." Lao Tzu calls this "embracing the one," by which the person "thereby becomes exemplar for all things under heaven." Here we're reminded that, by taking the one in our arms, perfection is open to us, and we need its blessings if we are to live our lives without being cut off from our full nature, if we are to discover new possibilities of meaning and joy. An athlete who seeks perfection through mastery of the game can open up to the embrace of the Way. Seeking the perfect jump shot is natural and in keeping with our nostalgia for the divine.

A perfect shot is a synchronous movement of our neural network, muscle fiber, bone and joints. It is a rhythmic vibration of energy extending from the brain to the various muscle systems of the body, from the feet through the legs, torso, arms, hands and finally through the fingertips at the release of the ball. The form—the combination of all the movements of the shot—is static at any instant but becomes dynamic as it changes from the crouch position through its intermediate motions up to the release.

The biochemical energy of the body imbues the form with its dynamism, creating an alchemical marriage of the masculine and feminine, giving birth to the flight of the ball as it ascends in its graceful arc to the basket. As the center of the ball meets the center of the rim, the perfection of the moment is realized. The shooter's body transmits an unbroken energy to the ball in a single unified flow. Perfection lies precisely in the unobstructed flow of cosmic energy, which is the ultimate nature of manifested reality.

We don't *arrive* at perfection since there's no fixed absolute point at which it occurs, but we can be part of its movement. The movement of perfection operates as love: a metaphysical infinite attraction that, like gravity in the physical world, draws all things back to their original center. It is an inner coitus, a marriage of heaven and earth, giving birth to the perfect human. This is the embracing of the Way through non-doing, action without idea, and it ends our inner division.

3

The Five-fold Movement

IN ORDER TO LEARN TO SHOOT A JUMP SHOT or diagnose problems that develop with good shooters in a slump, one has to break down the shot into its component movements. Within these categories, one can further subdivide each basic movement into its elements.

There are five major movements in executing a jump shot. Except for the fourth movement (the stroke), each flows into the next in a dynamic continuum. The first movement is the crouch, where the player lowers the body by bending at the knees so the trunk is inclined slightly and ends up at about a ninety-degree angle to the thighs. At this point, the body is momentarily poised up on the balls of the feet while the heels are raised slightly off the floor at an angle of approximately ten degrees to the horizontal. This foot position energizes the legs and upper body muscles for the second movement.

The body uncoils from the crouch position and extends to the point just before the athlete leaves the floor. This uncoiling displacement, the second movement, is similar to the uncoiling of a compressed spring. It allows the muscles of the body, primarily the leg muscles, to exert maximum force on the floor. Both the lower and upper body stretch upward while the legs and other muscle systems simultaneously push down on the floor. The player raises the ball upward at this time. The body's center of gravity must remain over the balls of the feet for balance as the body uncoils and inclines slightly forward. At the end of this second movement the heels rise up to about a forty-five-degree angle as the body straightens to an erect position before contact with the floor ends.

The third movement is the free flight vertical lift. As the body comes off the floor, the arms continue to extend upward, so the ball is centered over the ear. At this point of full upper body extension, the ball rests on the shooting hand's finger pad. The wrist is bent fully back so this hand now parallels the floor while the non-shooting hand is off to the side, lightly supporting the ball. The upper arm and forearm are perpendicular to each other. The head, neck, spinal column and legs are vertical, with the toes pointing almost straight down as the shooter approaches the top of the jump.

Now begins the fourth movement, the stroke. The stroke commences as the shoulder begins to rotate forward and the arm unfolds to the straight position; the arm is at an angle of about forty-five degrees to the horizontal. While the arm is coming forward, the wrist begins to rotate in the same direction. At full arm extension, the ball leaves the fingertips with a reverse rotation. After releasing the ball, the arm should momentarily be kept in the final release position, following the ball's initial path along the tangent to the arc or flight to the basket. This is the follow-through.

The fifth and final movement is the descent and landing. Although there is no special skill involved in having gravity bring you back to the floor, an imbalance in the landing often points to problems in the execution. Just as a gun recoils when a round leaves the muzzle, so too much recoil in the body indicates too much force and consequently a bad release. A good landing lets the shooter get back on defense or follow the shot quickly and gracefully.

Before analyzing where problems in shooting lie, one needs to have mastered all the elements of each major movement. Problems may and often do exist in several areas at the same time. Let's say a problem exists in the stroke. The shooter might not properly extend the arm before the release of the ball or might release the ball at an incorrect arc angle. To compensate for distance the shooter often pushes the ball instead of maintaining the purity of the stroke action. At the end of the stroke, the shooter might rotate the wrist to the right or to the left instead of directly forward. The shooter must also avoid excessive arm and leg force, insufficient backspin, and locking of the shoulder. Poor timing when releasing the ball, lack of proper gap between the palm and the ball, and lack of a full bend at the wrist will disrupt the basic shooting motion. One must understand proper technique perfectly to analyze problems effectively.

Mastery of technique is only one dimension of learning the art and science of shooting. In all Taoist or Zen arts, technical mastery is akin to training an animal in the sense that our brains and neuromuscular systems learn to work together to produce the correct gesture. The spontaneous dynamism and intelligence of the body itself is seen in such processes as the circulation of blood, the operation of the nervous systems, breathing and digestion. The functions of all bodily systems, except the reproductive organs, are to support muscle movement. Based on this, we can consider physical movement the ultimate function of our organism and expressive gesture the integration of body and mind.

When the bodily systems function freely on their own without the conceptual self interfering, the fundamental unconscious works in total harmony with our brain-body system. As strange as it may seem to those unaccustomed to thinking of American sports in terms of Eastern philosophy, the perfectly executed jump shot is a powerful illustration of the free-flowing energy of the Tao. If unhindered, the fundamental unconscious turns the seemingly pedestrian jump shot into an "artless art."

Just as no two things in the universe are exactly alike, no two jump shots can be exactly alike. Sometimes the principles of execution are nearly identical, but cosmic energy manifested through the individual places its unique stamp on every jump shot. Each player must attempt to make every shot identical within the unique form based on the principles of the five-fold movement.

4

The Still Point of the Cosmic Wheel

ALTHOUGH THE JUMP SHOT IS A DYNAMIC movement of energy, there is one unique point, a nearly measureless instant, during which the athlete remains frozen in space. This is both a culminating and germinating point. It ends the shooter's upward lift while simultaneously giving birth to the arc the ball traverses on its way to the rim. The point of release, born in a moment of stillness, gives flight to the ball with minimum force, just as the caterpillar immobilizes itself in the chrysalis before emerging as a beautiful butterfly.

In this regard, it is interesting to reflect on how the Taoist sage is said to sit at the "still point of the cosmic wheel." The cosmic wheel represents incessant change, the birth and death of all things. The center is the unique point of the wheel since it doesn't move. It symbolizes the "unmoved mover" of Aristotle, the still point of the moving energy that gives birth to all things.

Those of us who aren't Taoist sages fear the immobilization of our inner states because we cherish our emotions. But these inner movements knot our energy and prevent the "birth within" that Zen calls satori and the Taoist calls awakening to the "axis of the Tao." The axis of a sphere, like the center of a circle, is the locus of immovable points around which rotation takes place. A sage is not emotionless, but he or she doesn't seek security by trying to grasp something permanent in the flux of an eternally dynamic universe, and so is able to feel without being constricted by a consciousness limited to thought.

Most of us are attached to the movements of our psychological states—the stream of forms—an attachment that displaces our center. Our conscious states are like fireworks that are visible to our mind's eye; since they're so vivid, so compelling, we assume they're our true life, like the ups and downs experienced by characters in a novel. These charged spectacles of our inner life are similar to the specks of light seen by a prospector panning for gold in the only stream he knows. His aspirations rise continually, but each time he meets the same disappointment, fool's gold. Our emotional expectations and ruminations are fool's gold because they never resolve the problems of our suffering and conflicts. The Buddhist refers to these forms as *samskaras*; the psychoanalyst calls them complexes. Whatever we name them the result is the same: our energy hemorrhages.

This hemorrhaging can stop if we shift our attention from the forms of our consciousness—these images of everyday distress—to the nonformal, dimensionless center of our being. The doing or action of this shift of our inner eye is essentially a non-doing, because we are not interfering with or attempting to change our state in a conscious way. We are simply redirecting our attention. This actionless action brings us to the "asylum of rest," a safe haven, an inner palace where our inner immobility saves us from the painful disintegration of our energy.

When we look into the still center, our attention shifts directly toward the invisible source of our illusory thinking, called the "cave of phantoms" in Zen. Normally our attention is seized by forms, just as in a movie theater we face the screen on which the forms of the film are projected. Now, instead, we turn away from the screen and look toward the projector. This shift of our attention is a transformation, a passing beyond the forms of our consciousness that would destabilize and tear apart our inner world. Yet turning away from the screen of our formal consciousness, unlike looking toward the projector, does not blind us with the light.

Reaching this haven of the still center often brings us an unforeseen feeling of loss or sadness. We leave the circumference of the wheel—the wheel of the birth and death of our energy—and return to the still center. We can do this only for a moment, but it is enough to break the vicious cycle of our energy loss. With nothing to hold onto, our attention immediately reverts back to the forms of our consciousness. Our inner work must proceed with what the Buddha considered one of the cardinal virtues, patience. We continue with our normal living, shifting our attention to our true, dimensionless center when possible. One day we may arrive at the final release from our *samskaras* in what Zen calls satori and the Hindu calls *moksha*—liberation.

A shooter who tunes into the quiet inner center and times his or her jump shot correctly will release the ball at the top of the jump—the still point of the motion—realizing the possibilities of stillness in energy. In the still center, recognition of a deeper reality becomes possible. As the psalmist of the Old Testament tells us: "Be still and know that I am God."

5

Effortless Virtuosity

UNDERSTANDING THE RIGHTFUL PLACE of effort in our lives requires us to distinguish where it is useful and where it brings conflict. One particular kind of effort, the will to find the eternal in the ephemeral—to find a lasting satisfaction that nothing can threaten—lies hidden at the center of our inner being, and its effects on our lives are immense. Zen tells us we are slaves of this effort, this desire to exist. At first it seems absurd that we would need confirmation of such an obvious fact as existence. But this desire is getting at something deeper than merely the satisfaction of physical needs: we want *to be* in an absolute sense.

The genesis of this need to be, which exacts such great striving in our lives, is at the foundation of our psychological world. My fundamental unconscious knows intuitively that my true "I"—what the Vedanta calls the Self, Buddhism calls Buddha nature and Taoism calls the Tao—is the absolute ground not only of my being but of the universe. It is paradoxically my truest self and yet so vast and limitless it would be absurd to consider it something personal, something belonging to me. Yet my ego falsely assumes the attributes of this absolute ground—oneness, omniscience, omnipotence, immutability—as if it were personal and separable from the whole.

This inherent contradiction—along with the conflicts of life, the instability of experience and the inevitability of death—makes me doubt the absolute nature of my separate self. Nevertheless, I strive to confirm my personal divinity. I search for ways out of the impasse in order to free myself from this separated condition, but my efforts move me further in the direction of becoming—solidifying the trap of the isolated ego—and consequently are doomed to failure.

No phenomenal effort can satisfy a spiritual demand; experience that's rooted in striving is incapable of resolving the ego's struggle. We sense a void or state of nothingness at the core of our being, a kind of death or depression at the center of our inner life. In contrast, when the mind is quiet, without the slightest effort or movement—in a condition of "attention without object" and total sensitivity—we can awaken to a state beyond opposites. Here the spontaneous action of intelligence ends the illusory efforts "to be or not to be." Zen calls this "seeing into one's nature"—the actionless action of the Tao.

Not every expenditure of energy is necessarily the outcome of effort, although effort is necessary to accomplish certain tasks and learn new things. A ballerina spends years in daily practice to perfect her art. She exercises great efforts to have her body perform the fundamental gestures of ballet. When mastery develops, the greatest artists seem to move effortlessly. Once the techniques of the dance are mastered, the dancer can infuse her physical movements with the creative energy of her heart and soul. This freedom allows the love of dance to be expressed fully without effort getting in the way. Any hint of effort at this level would seem out of place.

In his sphere the shooter is a creative artist. Like the dancer, he faces
the trials and tribulations of artistic
mastery. It takes years to perfect the
form, timing and strength to execute
the shot at all feasible ranges from
the basket. Conceiving what is necessary in terms of form and strength
development, the shooter struggles to
perfect his coordination and timing.
Having mastered all the elements, he
functions in a state of effortlessness.

In 1981, a Brooklyn College pro-
fessor of physics named Peter Brancasio made a computer study using

no action

the laws of physics to analyze the different trajectories and
launching speeds necessary to make a successful jump shot. Up
until that time, not a single article had been published on the
physics of basketball. His research uncovered a startling fact
about shooting. Of all the trajectories that result in a successful
shot—and there are an indefinite number of them—one arc
stands out. He calls this arc the minimum force or minimum
speed trajectory. When a shooter is able to launch a shot at this
angle, he or she will sense that the shot feels effortless. This holds
true at all ranges from beyond the three-point line up to the rim.

When the ball is released with minimum force, the number
of arcs that can result in a successful shot increase dramati-
cally. In mathematical terms, the probability of making a basket
increases significantly. Brancasio adds, "The corresponding
launching speed for this shot (which is the lowest launching
speed for the given distance) provides the widest range of
launching angles for a successful shot." In other words, the highest percentage shot is the effortless shot, which would not sur-

prise any Taoist or Zen master. Good shooting is unforced, effortless technical virtuosity.

In the endeavor for self-understanding, effort can also be a hindrance and indication of conflict. We often respond to emotions and thoughts in terms of approval and disapproval, which make us imagine we can rid ourselves of negative qualities by applying effort—an act of will that can change what is to what should be. We think inner effortlessness leads to stagnation: "I have to struggle or else I'll vegetate." But as Krishnamurti says, "If we make an effort from the center of the self, it must inevitably produce more conflict, more misery." In fact, when the conflict of effort is absent, we discover a state of total energy.

Understanding an abstract problem also shows where effort and effortlessness are necessary. After breaking down a problem into its constituent elements, we often reach the solution in a state of release, a silence that allows the intelligence to operate apart from effort or desire for a solution. It is similar to a still pond where we can easily and clearly see the bottom. If we stir the waters, our vision will be limited. The inherent spontaneous action of the quiet mind is what the Taoists call *tzu-jan*. For this to operate, the mind's agitation, caused by our emotions and thoughts compounded by the effort to change them, must cease.

Right effort is the will to understand. If I love a sport, I understand practice is necessary. It is only struggle and conflict if I feel I should be doing something else or if I'm struggling for fame and recognition. For anything that's ultimately important in life—love, joy, creativity—effort is a thief disguised as a philanthropist.

6

Release

FROM TIME IMMEMORIAL people have sought release from the inherent suffering and death that define so much of human life. Something deep within us — our latent awareness of our infinite mind — tells us our lives don't have to be subject to what Hamlet calls "the whips and scorns of time."

All religions address this fundamental problem of releasing ourselves from the existential knots of the soul and seek to give us the key to the timeless dimension within that will free us from suffering and death. Jesus told us in effect that "unless a man dies, he will not be reborn."

In India, *moksha*—liberation—provides the solution to this existential dilemma. It requires years of study and the practice of ascetic disciplines such as yoga to free the soul from the prison of existence. Buddha was born into the philosophical and ascetic traditions of India, which were already at least a thousand years old before his birth. He found that most of the methods and ideas of his time had lost their validity and become mere formalisms without any living substance. Taking it upon himself to resolve the condition of human suffering, he wandered for years, searching for a solution. He engaged in the wide range of disciplines available in the world, but to no avail.

One day, weary of his relentless search, he realized the extreme practices he had undertaken brought him closer to death but that even physical death was not an ultimate solution to the problem of human suffering. Sitting himself under the now-famed Bodhi tree, he vowed not to move until the problem was solved. All night (or for seven nights, by some accounts) he sat confronting inner demons—all the doubts, fears and cravings that trap us in the difficulties of our lives—until finally he had shed the last restraint. He lifted his eyes to the rising sun and instantly experienced enlightenment.

This realization or existential transformation, whether called *moksha*, satori, enlightenment or something else, always results in a release from our present limited perception of reality and an entrance into a new dimension that ends all suffering. This release is the foundation and aim of the Buddha's teachings, which became known as the Middle Way for their reliance on methods, available to everyone, that develop attention and insight without recourse to extreme deprivations or indulgences.

Buddha's teachings spread to China, where they fused with Taoism and developed into Chan, which emphasizes the suddenness of release or enlightenment. According to this perspective, one does not *become* enlightened: our fundamental nature is already perfect just as it is. However, we are asleep to our "original nature." Hence, we use the term "awakening" to indicate release from the limitations of our formal consciousness with its inherent attachments, restlessness, fear, conflicts and suffering. This radical teaching of a sudden awakening, an immediate seeing into one's nature, taught by the Chan masters, spread to Korea and then into Japan, where it is called Zen.

The Zen form of Buddhism has influenced all the arts of Japanese culture: gardening, archery, calligraphy, flower arranging, serving tea, wrestling, fencing. Although release from limitations, attachments and suffering is the essential condition of all the arts inspired by Buddhism and Taoism, it is particularly critical and symbolic in archery. Releasing the bowstring is a measure both of pure technique and of the mental state of the archer. The string must be released unintentionally, by the fundamental unconscious.

The unconscious in Chan or Zen is not like the unconscious in our modern psychiatry—that is, the repository of unassimilated images and primeval forces. To the contrary, it is the intrinsic source of reality itself.

Years of practice and hard work are necessary for the archer to be able to release the arrow without interference from the ego. The dissolution of the bonds of the ego—our conscious pretense of controlling our acts—allows our unconscious principle to work its miracle. When the archer senses that the bowstring has released itself, he can't explain why or how it happened, though the teachings of Zen make him aware of the cosmic significance of this seemingly personal and ordinary act.

Like the release of the arrow, the release of a jump shot is both the pinnacle of achievement from an aesthetic point of view and the proof of mastery of the mechanics of shooting from an athletic perspective. At the release of the ball, two primary factors determine whether the ball will enter the basket: departing speed and departing angle. The speed of the ball leaving the shooter's hand is determined by the various muscle systems in the body. The angle of launch is largely set by the slight upward angle of shoulder rotation that results in the arm's final extension at an angle of approximately forty-five degrees to the horizontal. At the final point of release, the wrist angle should also be at approximately forty-five degrees to the horizontal as the ball comes off the fingertips. A good final release feels as if it has occurred on its own, and the shooter knows intuitively and immediately with a considerable certainty whether the shot will fall.

Within the complex gesture of the release, the shooter experiences a sense of inherent mystery. He feels a good release as a surprise and as something that's occurred on its own. Neurologists can trace the nervous and muscular systems involved, but they have no idea where in the human body or brain this marvelous feat of the organism comes together.

The Tao creates by becoming empty. Just as a flower suddenly opens to the sky, the release emerges from the true source and fundamental center of all things. As Lao Tzu said, "There was something undefined and complete coming into existence before Heaven and Earth. How still it was and formless, standing alone, and undergoing no change, reaching everywhere and in no danger of being exhausted. It may be regarded as the mother of all things." The ultimate controller of the shot is not an "I" or conventional self with a name and psychological history, but the Self or Tao that governs the cosmic movement of atoms, cells and stars as well as the simplest human gesture.

7

The Containment of Form

ONE OF THE FOREMOST PRINCIPLES of the ancient Chinese exercise art of tai chi chuan is containment, which implies both harmony and efficiency. Harmony refers to an integration of mind and body, and efficiency implies no wastage of energy in the execution of a gesture. According to tai chi chuan, a flowing, arcing movement provides containment—the spontaneous control of any physical skill—by limiting the excessive force typical of such jerky and angular acts as punching or kicking. Shooting a basketball, whether a jump shot, hook, push shot or finger roll, requires this containment—an efficient, graceful and accurately articulated gesture.

The jump shot involves movements and principles common to all shots, but each shot has its unique aspects. Consider the two basic hook shots: the sky hook and the sweeping hook. In both, the shooter is positioned so that a line extended through his shoulders bisects the rim. For the sky hook, the shooting arm is held straight up, parallel to the side of the body. In both hooks, the ball rests on the finger pad of the shooting hand, which is fully bent back at the wrist. The shooter releases the ball by rotating the wrist forward while the arm remains in its original position. The principle of containment—as practitioners of tai chi express it, "The curve embraces the straight"—exists in the curvilinear rotation of the wrist. In the case of the sweeping hook, the arm is initially straight out at about a forty-five-degree angle to the vertical, then rotates forward to the basket. The ball is released by a rotation at the wrist when the arm reaches the straight-up position. In executing either shot, the shooter rolls the ball off the fingertips with a reverse rotation. Again, we observe the principle of containment, "the finding of the straight in the curve."

The principle of the curve embracing the straight also figures in the push shot and the finger roll, shots significantly different from the hook shots. In the push shot, the curve is in the circular motion of the overall movement. Consider the typical buzzer-beating, mid-court desperation shot, and you can visualize the basic motion of the push shot. The shooter holds the ball about a foot above the waist, resting it on the heel of the palm. The shooting arm moves up and out in a continuous circular motion. When the arm is fully extended at an angle of about forty-five degrees above the horizontal, the wrist is bent backwards, and the ball is released with a forward turn of the wrist, which imparts a reverse rotation. The finger roll is a shot where the extended or bent arm can be at nearly any angle to the basket. Again, the ball rolls off the finger pad by rotation at the wrist.

Finally, for the jump shot, the circular action of the stroke while the arm straightens provides containment up to the point of release. In a manner resembling the release of the arrow in Zen archery, the jump shot employs the muscles of the forearm, wrist and fingers, which supply the launching force needed to release the ball. The prime function of the arm and shoulder is to guide and align the shot. The upward and forward movements of the arm counterbalance the inertia of the arm itself. These complementary conditions give rise to the circular motion of the stroke. According to Taoism, the way of heaven operates through the dynamic interplay of active and passive principles.

The principle of containment is general: it applies to all shots. By having the curve embrace the straight, containment prevents the "brick," a shot released with excessive force and little or no touch. For the shooter, the way of heaven is the way of the stroke.

8

The Purity of a Pure Shooter

THE QUEST FOR PURITY IS A QUEST for simplicity. According to
Jewish and Christian traditions, we lost our purity and the
simplicity of our Edenic state when Adam ate from the tree of
knowledge of good and evil. Our fall from grace suggests we
have incorporated inner complications contrary to our original
pure state. The modern idea of progress, as applied to our psychological world, implies we're becoming something other than
our "original nature," which traditionally is a reflection of God.
This is the fall into multiplicity and attachment that Christians
and Jews call sin and Buddhists call ignorance.

The idea of evolution in the natural world parallels this idea
of progress in the material world. Both are characterized by their
ceaseless movement toward a better future. Besides contradict-
ing the fundamental law of entropy in physics—a law stating
that for any organized system the arrow of time always points
in the direction of disorder—both ideas encourage a mentality
beset by a dispersion into fragmented multiplicity without the

balance of simplicity, unity and purity. In order to understand the clarity of light shining within, we need to recover the soul's primal nature of emptiness. This requires a detachment from time and from the image-making mental processes that lead to continual distraction. Our distractedness disables the purifying ablution of total attention.

In Taoism, it is exactly the purification of the mind and its attendant silence that allows the action of the Tao. In their writings, Taoists use the metaphor of the "spiritual mirror" to indicate that the mind, in some mysterious way, only reflects what arises from its infinite depths. As Meister Eckhart said, "The soul contemplates itself in the mirror of divinity. God Himself is the mirror, which He conceals from whom He will, and uncovers to whom He will. . . . The more the soul is able to transcend all words, the more it approaches the mirror. In this mirror union occurs as pure undivided likeness."

Physically, a shooter fulfills the ideal of purity by transforming complex action into simple motions. He or she must isolate and master the muscles necessary for the spontaneous, unhindered flow of the shot. The body's ability to control itself without improper mixing of muscle systems results in a shooting flow that appears, despite years of practice, to be unlearned. Great neuromuscular complexity has the outward appearance of pure simplicity and grace.

Laziness, the body's tendency to take the easy way by mixing improper muscle systems or ignoring the principles of optimum form (as discussed in Chapter Three) prevents the shooter from realizing purity. The most common error in shooting is precisely the impurity of unnecessary complexity, the improper mixing of stroke and push shot motions. Although this can occur at any range, it becomes especially evident at relatively far distances from the basket. The shooter compensates for distance by using the pushing strength of the full arm rather than relying on the primary muscles of the fingers, wrist and forearm, contaminating the pure stroking action. Such a poorly executed shot appears jerky.

Mental concepts during the shooting act contaminate the pure flow of the shot. In Zen archery and swordsmanship, the release of the arrow and the movement of the sword need to happen on their own without concepts obstructing the action. The absence of ego is paramount. A well-executed jump shot occurs unimpeded, like clear and flowing water, itself the great symbol of purity.

9

The Principle of Extension

SPATIAL EXTENSION IS FUNDAMENTAL to the game of basketball. Unconscious awareness of the principle of extension—the quantitative lengthening of distance in both vertical and horizontal directions in order to elude the defense—led to the spontaneous development of the jump shot nearly sixty years ago.

In shooting the jump shot, the arm isn't held straight up. Instead, the forearm and upper arm make a ninety-degree angle at the elbow with the ball positioned on the finger pad above the head, centered over the ear. At this position, the elbow is about at eye level. As the arm uncoils, the ball is released at full extension.

This extension improves accuracy. The higher the ball is at the time of release, the greater the chance it will go in. Extending the ball at a maximum comfortable distance over the head lets a six-foot guard release the ball from a higher point than a seven-foot center who shoots the ball from about ear level with hardly any vertical leap. (Many tall players shoot a modified one-hand set shot and call it their jump shot.) Maximum horizontal arm extension is also necessary, so at the point of release the arm is straight, at a forty-five-degree angle above the floor.

Other shots also benefit from this principle. The first shot that made full use of extension was the sky hook, a shot during which the arm is totally outstretched in the vertical plane and the ball is released off the finger pad from this point of elevation. The shot on the move, often referred to as a runner, illustrates maximum vertical extension. In this shot, the player moves the ball at high speed and suddenly picks up the dribble with one leg raised so the upper leg or thigh is perpendicular to the lower leg or calf. With the other foot still on the floor and the entire body extended upward on the ball of the foot, the shooter releases the ball at full arm extension. The graceful finger roll, a shot similar to the runner but occurring closer to the rim, is also released at full arm extension, the arm reaching toward the basket as if making a ritual offering to the gods. The ball floats off the fingertips.

The principle of extension plays a significant role in offensive team strategy. For freedom of movement, the five players should extend themselves in width and in depth, forcing the defense to spread out. This gives the offensive team the spatial extension needed to run set plays with minimal defensive constriction. In addition, it provides the ball carrier the opportunity and freedom to create his own offense, since the only defensive barrier on the way to the basket is the player guarding him. Some of the most spectacular moves in all of sports are performed, one on one, when the offensive team adheres to the principle of extension.

Since extension is so crucial, we could easily conclude that basketball is primarily a game of quantity. Considering our general inclination to reduce all things to number, it's important to reflect here on the Taoist teaching that all phenomena arise from the union of the active and passive perfections. These perfections combine to create all pairs of complementary opposites, including quantity and quality. Although both quantity and quality describe the manifested universe, they correspond respectively to earth, which in Taoist reckoning refers only to the physical world, and to heaven, which is not subject to the limitations of measurement. Earth is material and heaven intangible.

Seeing life in terms of quantity alone is an error that leads to a lack of proportion in judgment. Even if the Bible tells us, "God ordered all things in measure, number, and weight," this certainly doesn't mean reality can or should be reduced to quantity alone. In theology and metaphysics, one can speak of divine attributes or qualities. Surely it would be a mistake to try measuring or numbering these.

Number in itself is pure quantity, stripped of every qualitative aspect. Nothing in reality can exist in a condition that lacks the dimension of quality. Number by nature is discontinuous and separative, and creates a tendency toward uniformity by reducing things to units. Discontinuity and separation can lead to the denial of wholeness, and uniformity denies creativity.

In basketball, this leads to dull and repetitive offensive and defensive strategies. We can observe similar consequences in most endeavors. W. Edwards Deming, a respected business consultant, points out that wrongly used numerical analysis in areas such as merit systems, rankings of people, and measures of quality and numerical goals brings about a stifling corporate climate that leads precisely to an inflexible uniformity.

Many divisions of number and reason have no real existence. Suppressing qualitative aspects in any activity ignores the heavenly dimension because it mistakes uniformity for unification. It substitutes the relative utility of separation for a complete understanding.

The qualitative pole of reality is always the most complex and sometimes even the least in quantity. The acorn produces the great oak, the single fertilized egg produces the billions of muscle, nerve, bone and all other cells of the body. The qualitative pole brings us to the fundamental mystery at the center of all things.

Extension as form is qualitative. The form of a body is the shape of the surface that defines its volume. Although we can measure the area and volume of any shape, this doesn't mean shape is simply quantitative. A pyramid can have the same volume as a rectangular solid, but we can't say they are the same in any way except numerically. Because of the qualitative aspects of shape, no two objects can be exactly alike.

Geometry, the mathematics of form, has many qualitative dimensions, especially as it engages the human spirit. A great work of art or architecture often awakens in us the sense of beauty because of its order, balance, coherence and form—attributes that are qualitative in nature—and brings us closer to our essential core.

The qualitative aspect of extension also applies to space itself as an assembly of defined directions. Size is the quantitative aspect of space and direction is its qualitative counterpart. Underlying *feng shui*, the Taoist-based art of harmonizing structures, people and the environment, is this same principle of nature. Environments are ordered to take advantage of the qualitative dimension of space. *Feng shui* literally means wind and water, which symbolize the active and passive principles. *Feng shui* provides principles for arranging space in order to balance yin and yang in any environment.

In Taoism, as in Buddhism, void is form and form is void: a simple way of understanding this statement is by observing how the empty space within and surrounding an object is what gives it form, while at the same time "form" is an abstract idea and therefore empty of substance. Although the extension of the body during the jump shot—the distance of the balls of the feet to the outstretched fingers—can be measured quantitatively, its essence, its form, is qualitative. It is precisely this qualitative side of extension as form that lends beauty, grace and intelligence to the sport of basketball. Ultimately, form is a ripple on the ocean of emptiness. The movement of energy as form, expressed when extending for a jump shot, is like the flight of the eagle that leaves no trace on the infinite sky of emptiness.

10

Centering

THE CONCERN WITH CENTERING is a universal attribute of human existence. The connection of a center with the origin of the universe is seen in our great religious traditions. In the book of Proverbs we read, "He has set his compass on the face of the deep," and the Rig Veda states, "with his ray he has measured heaven and earth." A point is a dimensionless geometric object that has no property but location. All of space can be visualized as emanating from a point at the center of three intersecting, perpendicular lines that represent length, width and depth. These lines form six rays, radii whose extension from the center forms a sphere of indefinite extent.

The center as the unique point—all other points are equidistant from it—is symbolic of the *logos* or divine Word in Christianity, of the invariable middle in the actionless action of the Tao, of the Divine Station in Islam and of the *ain sof* or Infinite in Jewish mysticism. In physics, the transcendent point of generation is the center of the big bang theory's origin of the universe. It is called the initial singularity, which doesn't exist in space-time but is the source out of which the universe emerged. The idea of a center resonates with the mystery and order of creation. All life revolves around a center that eludes our conscious grasp.

Even in our secular world, concern with the idea of a center arises frequently. Half a century ago Americans placed a commemorative stone at Lebanon, Kansas, marking the exact center of the continental United States. In ancient and more traditional civilizations, a location considered to possess both physical and spiritual qualities was marked by a stone referred to as the *omphalos*, Greek for "the navel of the world." This stone symbolized the cosmic pole that supports the entire universe, just as the navel in the human body is the approximate center of gravity of the entire organism. In a sense, the navel is the point of origin of our entry into the world.

Every great religion has a geographic location that for it represents the sacred center of the universe: Jerusalem for Jews and Christians, Mecca for Muslims, Benares for Hindus. The Chinese called their entire country "The Middle Kingdom" and the Egyptians referred to theirs as Chemia, the "Heart of the World." Although many of these locations are not geographically central, they represent spiritual and metaphysical points where heaven and earth come together.

Just as any object in space has these three perpendicular axes—length, width and depth—so the human body has a transverse axis through the hips, a median axis from front to back and a longitudinal axis from head to toe. These axes divide the body symmetrically and meet at the center of gravity of the body.

The center of gravity of any body is the average position of weight. If you know the location an object's center of gravity, you can balance the object on this single point. In human terms, a man's center of gravity is about an inch below his navel; a woman's is slightly lower, since most women are wider at the

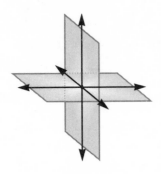

hips and men are wider at the shoulders. In either case it's about midway between front and back. If the body is bent into a different shape, the center of gravity moves. With certain body shapes, the center of gravity is actually outside the body. You can test this by standing against a wall. Keeping your heels and buttocks touching the wall, bend over and try to touch your toes. You find yourself falling over because your center of gravity is outside your body at a point in front of you, not over your feet, your base of support. Clearly if you're to maintain a state of equilibrium your center of gravity must be over your feet.

When shooting the jump shot, the first movement is to lower the body's center of gravity by bending at the knees, lowering the buttocks and raising the heels off the floor about ten degrees. The whole weight of the body is now on the balls of the feet. Here the flexion of the feet energizes the leg muscles. The torso should be approximately perpendicular to the thighs at the lowest point of the crouch and the body's center of gravity should be over the balls of the feet.

As the body extends from the crouch position to the erect position, the center of gravity moves upward while the heels rise to about forty-five degrees off the floor. The center of gravity now moves slightly forward over the toes. While the body uncoils to the erect position, the ball also moves upward. After the body leaves the floor, both the body's center of gravity and the ball continue to rise. The center of gravity, or geometrical center, of the ball should be over the ear when the arm is fully extended over the head.

The more the body's center of gravity rises from the bottom of the crouch to the point of maximum lift from the ground, the greater the vertical leap. This re-emphasizes the importance of extending the ball above head level to raise the center of gravity vertically. Just by stretching his arms straight above his head, the shooter's center of gravity moves upward two to three inches.

Extending and balancing the center of gravity pay multiple dividends. When the arm is fully extended, or when the forearm and upper arm are at about ninety degrees, the center of gravity of the ball and body should be in the same vertical plane. This balances the body when in the air. The aligned centers of gravity now form a vertical axis that provides stability the same way the axis of the Tao or the tree of heaven links all things together in a universal and total harmony.

11

The Gap

WHEN ONE REFLECTS on the immense harmonic and vibratory system of the universe, it may first appear that there's a continuum from the simplest hydrogen atom and biological cell to the huge mammals and plants to vast galaxies. But if we look closely at this seemingly continuous universe—the "ten thousand things" of Taoism—we find three distinct domains separated by two gaps.

The first defining gap is between the inanimate, lifeless or mineral domain and the animate domain of plants and animals. The next is between the animate plane and the intellectual plane characterized by language. These three planes represent a clear hierarchy, since each plane above the inanimate integrates the plane or planes below it. It is interesting to observe that humans are the sole integrators of all three domains, since we contain the inanimate elements (oxygen, carbon, calcium, etc.); the animate processes of respiration, circulation, the life and death of cells and so forth; and intellect.

In the microcosm of the atom, we also find discrete jumps when an atom absorbs or emits energy. At the beginning of the twentieth century, the prevailing theories assumed that any substance could absorb a continuous stream of energy. But scientists discovered that, to the contrary, a substance could only absorb or emit a finite amount of energy, called the quantum.

These examples let us hint at a more profound gap that can only be pointed to, not defined with language, since it occurs beyond the domain of the intellect. This gap, an abyss between relative reality (the phenomenal world) and absolute reality (the realm of non-being), is the last obstacle on the way to experiencing what in Taoism is called the Great Awakening. For more than a thousand years, Zen masters have told their students to jump into the abyss—only by taking this leap can we realize ultimate reality. But what abyss are they referring to? Not the gap between the inanimate, animate or intellectual domains of manifested, relative reality. It's more like what the physicist Henry Strapp says about nature: "Everything we know about nature is in accord with the idea that the fundamental process of nature lies outside space-time . . . but generates events that can be located in space-time."

The gap is an essential attribute of the Tao, requiring the death of the relative self or ego for the Way to operate in the life of an individual. Although the Tao is simultaneously immanent and transcendent in creation, there can be no continuum between absolute and relative reality. That the Tao can exhibit the opposite attributes of immanence and transcendence should not be surprising. This heavenly archetype is reflected in the laws of quantum mechanics, where particles can be in opposite states simultaneously. For example, atoms can have both vertical and horizontal spin axes, and a photon is both a wave and a particle.

In its transcendence, the Tao has three attributes our mind can conceive of but not perceive. Fundamentally, the absolute is "bottomless and empty," as Lao Tzu tells us. It is non-being or *wu-chi* in Chinese. From it comes pure being, or *tai chi*, some-times called the "great extreme." And heaven and earth, the pri-mordial pair, issue forth from it. Though we describe these at-tributes separately, they are not distinct entities.

Between heaven and earth there is a discontinuity or gap. Like the particles in the quantum world, this gap expresses the complementary conditions of both uniting and separating the action of heaven and earth. It is a gap from our point of view in manifestation. Its opposite qualities are analogous to the quan-tum particles — protons, electrons, atoms and photons — that find definition in a particular state when we observe them. When we think about the gap, we collapse it into its separative mode. Simply put, it is only a gap for us. It is not a gap for the absolute in its omniscience.

In the Tao of the jump shot, the gap between the ball and the palm of the shooter's hand is critically important. This gap or void, although empty and non-acting, provides the condition of a proper and effective reverse spin to the ball. From the stand-point of physics, if a rotating sphere is moving forward yet has a reverse spin, when it makes contact with a surface both the spinning and translational motions decrease significantly. For a shooter, this means the ball will decrease its speed, spin and en-ergy if it hits the rim or backboard. The slowing action improves the chance of a favorable bounce that could make the differ-ence between a score and a missed shot.

Along with the gaps inherent in the nature of things, there is an illusory separation. This gap exists as long as one is not awak-ened or enlightened. It makes us see the world in terms of an "I" opposed to a "non-I." All doctrines of Eastern philosophy and psychology address themselves to abolishing this illusory gap. The opposition comes from separating the thinking proc-ess into a thinker cut off from thought, an observer separated from the observed. Consequently, the "I" as subject divides itself from all things, inner and outer. This illusory gap between the thinker and the thought is a hindrance to the shooter, breaking rhythm and interrupting the flow. When the shooter overcomes the hindrance and leaps into the abyss, heaven and earth unite.

12

The Accuracy of Aimlessness

ONE OF THE PROBLEMS IN UNDERSTANDING the teachings of Taoism and Zen is their insistence that the Tao is the aimless and evidently purposeless life of the eternal present. For most people, this is a difficult concept. After all, living is a serious activity fraught with problems of raising and educating children, earning money and getting ahead. In the midst of all this, we face the constant threat of illness, downturns in the economy, loss of employment, war, poverty, crime, terrorism, cravings of many kinds, environmental destruction, ethnic, racial, marital and general human conflicts and other forms of suffering. Some of these problems are inherent in the general movements of the world and the age we find ourselves in. Others are a direct result of the well-intentioned goals of human beings, whose fragmentary approach to existence multiplies problems instead of solving them.

If we want a solution, we would do well to consider the simple and humble life of the ancient itinerant and monastic sage, who infused culture and society with a creative energy, a spirit of harmony and peace, devotion to nature, compassion, nonviolence, and noble ideals that ignited the arts, sciences and general well being of the people whose lives were blessed by the seemingly radical teaching of aimlessness.

Our lives and society depend entirely on the ethic of achievement based on a presumption of purpose. Can we let ourselves hear the Taoist teaching of nonattainment, nonachievement and aimlessness? To do so we have to make a distinction between the necessary plans and goals associated with activities such as building a house or planning a trip to Mars and the psychological dimension projected into setting goals. This projection is an attempt to grasp something intangible such as security, pleasure, power, or the confirmation of our being from experience. Simply put, we are trying to improve ourselves through experience. Our pursuits of riches and fame attempt to compensate for a lack of the Tao in our lives.

Our fundamental need is for what Christians call salvation and Buddhists call enlightenment. Lao Tzu's insistence on poverty of purpose is an antidote to the quest for self-fulfillment, which only leads to suffering. He knew that the state of non-striving was not one of morose listlessness but one of pure energy unfettered by selfish aims. Aims and goals are always of tomorrow—didn't Jesus admonish us to take no thought of the morrow? Didn't he tell us to be poor in spirit?

In Zen archery, the master always chides the student for aiming his shots and for feeling disdain or pride concerning failure and success. One master responded to an anxious student by saying, "The Great Doctrine holds this to be sheer devilry. It knows nothing of a target which it sets up at a definite distance from the archer. It only knows of the goal which cannot be aimed at technically, and it names this goal, if it names it at all, the Buddha. . . . So too the archer hit the target without having aimed—more I cannot say."

This is perfect advice for a basketball player seeking to improve her shooting even though she may not be consciously interested in the spiritual possibilities of satori. Many players, not understanding the formless intelligence that infuses skilled gestures (and the universe as a whole) are under the impression that a shot must be aimed at the basket. To the contrary, one doesn't aim a football, baseball or basketball but rather releases it by allowing unconscious, formless intelligence and neuromuscular memory to work on their own.

Consciousness as thought interferes with the execution of any gesture. We don't think about the movements of our legs when walking. Consider the immense complexity of the action-reaction sequences among the brain, nervous system and muscles required for a jump shot. The contraction and extension of hundreds of muscles during the crouch, stretch, lift, stroke and final release of the ball are ultimately controlled in the cerebral cortex, the topmost brain layer, which is critical for thought. Visual signals from the environment—the positions of opposing players and teammates, distance from and angle to the basket—resonate within the brain's field of awareness. Each muscle has a different pathway and different cortical cells control its movement. The cortical cells send out a signal through a fiber that extends to the medullary cells in the spinal column, which links up with more than six hundred muscle systems. This vast network is far more complicated than all the telecommunications networks in the world, constantly switching some cells on and some off during the shooting process.

The only part our formal consciousness plays in the jump shot or in any other skilled gesture is the thought command we give to make it happen. There is nothing in the brain that can be identified as the physical location corresponding to this command. Here we have stepped outside the physical domain and entered the subtle domain.

In this way, a jump shot is unconsciously or aimlessly executed. By mastery of alignment, shooting becomes spontaneous and beyond conscious control. By keeping the shooting arm in a plane parallel with the side of the body, the shooter will release the ball, and as long as the wrist movement is correct, the ball won't fall to the right or left of the rim. An imaginary line extending from the elbow should bisect the center of the rim. This alignment is similar to the sights on a gun. Launching speed and launching angle determine whether the shot falls long or short. This is set by neuromuscular memory and immediate perception.

Our entire organism is designed for action. The slightest gesture is pure miracle, with roots beyond conscious control in what is called the fundamental unconscious. Mastery of form combined with a mental awareness allows and provides the accuracy of aimlessness.

SECOND HALF

13

The Moon in the Water

BUDDHISTS HAVE A METAPHOR OF "the moon in the water" that signifies the instantaneous response of the mind's essence to physical reality. As soon as the moon appears in the sky, its image reflects in the water. The moon here represents any physical stimulus and the water represents the mind. This metaphor points to the immediacy of perception: the act of perceiving occurs instantly and spontaneously, not as the result of a human being thinking about something and then acting.

The immediate perception ideally translates into physical action as a lightning response, which in the ancient art of swordsmanship was indispensable to all technique and often the difference between life and death. The mind of the swordsman had to be so alert and sensitive that he was aware of an opponent who came from an angle not visually perceptible.

There are references in the ancient writings on swordsmanship that describe the proper state of mind in terms of the sword itself. Here the sword, a physical object, melts into the Tao, which flows without obstruction. The masters called this state "the sword of mystery" and the "sword of no abode." Mystery here means indescribability rather than incomprehensibility. A word classifies an entity, a process or an action in contrast to what it is not. Mind as mystery is beyond the duality of classification and beyond words, but certainly capable of being understood. The "sword of no abode" points to a mind limitless in depth. Its primary response is immediate and direct and has nothing to do with ideas.

In athletics, for the most part, we have reduced quickness to the number of fast twitch muscles an athlete possesses. However, it's obvious that the physically quickest players don't necessarily excel in what we call anticipation and "reading" the court or field. These qualities are mental. We can learn about anticipation from the metaphors of "the moon in the water" and "the swords of mystery and no abode." By understanding the mental aspects of quickness and fluidity, we can improve our reaction time and overall responsiveness.

Suppose you are standing on the sidelines watching two teams scrimmage and a player unexpectedly throws the ball at your head. Out of the corner of your eye, you see the ball coming. Immediately, two practically simultaneous yet successive things occur. First, energy bursts forth from an invisible fountain within you while your arm rises up to block the ball. The perception of the oncoming ball, the welling up of your energy and the blocking of the ball are dynamically linked in a fluid response.

The birth of this energy from a seemingly invisible fountain at the center of your being demonstrates that your organism conceals an intelligent energy source that responds immediately in a way perfectly adapted to the external world. This energy is certainly not the Freudian *id*, the blind and brutish energy tying us to the swamp or jungle from which we supposedly evolved. This awakened energy is initially informal and obviously beyond conscious thought. It responds to the outside world without con-

moon and water

scious approval or disapproval. It doesn't assume a division between the outside world and the perceiver.

However, after this instantaneous response of blocking the ball, images of the person who threw the ball begin to form. These thoughts, centering on the antagonist or "not-self," awaken new streams of energy from the invisible inner fountain that give rise to anger. These new streams are now directed against the person who threw the ball. The reaction is no longer the pure, spontaneous response of stopping the ball, since it involves the element of time, however minimal. You're no longer flowing with the fluidity of the original pure energy—instead you're resisting the birth of energy within, getting the urge to strike the perpetrator. This time-bound reaction doesn't come from the perpetrator as much as it comes from the awakened streams of energy within you.

Constant readiness requires total alertness of brain, mind and body. The instantaneous response is like striking a drum: the drum vibrates exactly according to how it was struck. This responsiveness isn't a blind return to wild instincts and impulses, which would be a reaction, not action. When we are in a state of heightened awareness, the birth of the organic energy from our vital source—a manifestation of the Tao—doesn't result in any secondary mental reaction. Our formless intelligence knows the world directly, outside the confines of the image-forming brain, and acts in accordance with the nature of things.

On the basketball court, a player needs to be in this constant state of alertness, where the entire organism flows without hindrance. "Getting up" for a game isn't really a question of emotions, which are fragmentary, but of evoking a state of pure energy from which the organism can respond totally and intelligently to the constant swirl of ever-changing game conditions.

Good jump shooters create their own offense precisely through this alertness. They must be able to move with and without the ball while continually trying to outmaneuver the defense by finding a gap, seam or open spot on the floor. If the ball is in their hands, they must see the relative positions of teammates and opposing players while also reading the reactions and tactics of the defenders. Dribbling with great dexterity, stopping on a dime, changing direction without hesitation, exploding quickly off the floor, "dishing" to an open teammate, avoiding the tendency to give up the dribble at inopportune moments, putting continued pressure on the defense, executing the "give and go," penetrating the defense, and maintaining offensive and defensive balance are complex skills that require immediate response. Game conditions vary constantly so the player must be like an intelligent nerve ending, instantly adjusting to an ever-changing panorama of situations.

When an athlete makes a move precisely suited to some difficult array of conditions, it seems to happen on its own. The manifested quickness and dexterity aren't a result of conscious thought, but an example of what Zen calls the controlled accident. The origin of the jump shot itself seems to have been a controlled accident, since no one knows who was the first to use it. Adolph Rupp, the great Kentucky coach, said it just burst in upon us from nowhere.

14

Shooter's Doubt and the Doubt of Being

DESPITE LIVING IN AN AGE WHERE science champions the certainty of empirical and rational methods, doubt reigns supreme in our hearts and souls. Humans are heirs of a doubt that no ideology can assuage, no identification with any group can end (though in some cases awareness and sensitivity to doubt can be silenced through the drug of illusion or the superficial comforts of daily routine).

The origin of this doubt is directly related to the way our psyche (our reasoning, feeling and will) develops. This development is gradual, from rudimentary sensory awareness in infancy to the most abstract reasoning in the teen years. Culture, parental conditioning and education shape our views of reality and the way our thinking responds to stimuli in the world around us.

The thinking brain develops its powers once the animal organism has predisposed it to form hidden assumptions about life and our place in the world. Abstract thought appears in an organism whose emotions and desires are already geared toward affirming individual primacy.

The intellectual function, revealed largely through language, differentiates us from other animals. This function, which permits pure, objective thought, begins to emerge when the child is under the influence of limiting impulses that attempt to set him or her apart from others. When the child first begins to speak, he utters "me, not you," affirming a partial and individual view of things. It takes patient explanation to have the child understand that other people and other circumstances can have precedence and intervene in attempts to satisfy our desires.

This childhood tendency to exclusively affirm the individual that begins in childhood should not blind us to the innocence, spontaneity and simplicity of the child's nature. Childhood remains a potent spiritual symbol and a precondition for returning to what Taoists call "the primordial state," or "the state of origins." Even so, our latent assumptions about life need to be understood, since the emergence of intellect becomes intertwined with the demands of the animal organism.

Abstract thought results in the notion of an "I," "me" or "self," dividing the organism in two parts, body and soul, soma and psyche, or "me" and "not-me." This formation of the "I-subject" creates a metaphysical assumption of enormous implications. It erects a barrier between the mind and its inner movements of emotion, desire and thought. This split between the "I" and reality ends up becoming a division between "self" and "other." Anything perceived as a threat to one's existence becomes part of a "not-self." Aspects of the body and thinking process can become part of this "not-self." One may deny negative thoughts and emotions such as doubt and fear, yet denial only inflames them.

The division into duality brings in its wake other subconscious assumptions and beliefs. We assume this "I" to be absolute, a miniature first cause, above the perpetual flux of cosmic reality. As any Taoist would say, where there is belief there must be its correlative doubt. Even before our pretensions reveal their flaws, this hidden doubt gnaws behind every interaction. Every significant thing we do has behind it Hamlet's "to be or not to be." We're like wayward pilgrims, constantly seeking confirmation of a subconscious belief that the relative is in fact the absolute. We want life to confirm the absurd hypothesis that this "self" is the center of all things.

Of course there's a partial truth in this assumption, since the center is within at the same time it's everywhere. But we can easily see that mind—as cosmic mind, the fundamental reality of all things—is not bound by this relative "I," but is the universal Self of the Vedanta or the "I am that I am" of Moses' revelation in the Old Testament.

If my shooting is in a slump I face a two-sided problem. Overtly, I face the practical problem of analyzing technique and game situations in order to correct any mechanical shortcoming. Simultaneously I face a hidden problem related to the "doubt of being" lurking subconsciously within my thoughts. It is here that I debate my illusory hypothesis, hoping I will receive confirmation of the absolute claim of my ego.

This futile endless debate between my being and my nothingness, between self and not-self, wastes my energy in useless conflict. The adversarial part the world plays when it denies the "I" is irreducible. Psychologically, this wreaks havoc with my so-called confidence. I become obsessed with ending my slump, which in turn increases inner pressure to perform.

This mental state denies the spontaneous action of the Tao. In other words, one interferes with the body's natural intelligence to perform the free-flowing gesture it has been trained to execute.

The slump of the athlete and its attendant "doubt-of-being" problem are no different than any other situation in life where one faces a perceived defeat. On the conscious level, a business owner facing the loss of critical sales or a person facing the loss of a spouse have definite practical problems to contend with. Attempts to deal with these practical problems are affected by subconscious patterns that distort these human setbacks into a defeat of the "self" and a triumph of the "not-self."

These situations appear as a specter of death or as absolute nothingness. This greatly disturbs our psychological equilibrium and can lead to severe depression or suicide. If we don't realize that these subconscious, illusory assumptions that the "self" should triumph absolutely over the "not-self" are fueling extreme reactions, then inappropriate responses to the practical challenges of life become complicated further. "For the man given up to doubt," says the Bhagavad Gita, "there is no salvation either in this world or the next." The slumping athlete, like the business owner and grieving spouse, is tangled in the throes of this doubt that can be transformed when the inner eye is opened by self-understanding.

15

Harmony

A JUMP SHOT BRINGS TOGETHER THE coordination of body and mind in a movement of complementary opposites we can call harmony—a balance or equilibrium expressed through rhythm and proportion, set apart from the causal world view of science. The harmonious movement of opposites exists at all levels of a shot's execution. In the overall vertical movement, the descending and ascending motion of the crouch and stretch complement the lift and descent. In the transverse or horizontal plane, the stroke has both coiling and uncoiling actions.

This equilibrium is particularly evident at the moment of release, when the exertion of great muscle strength, coordination and balance give way to a sense of effortlessness. The flight of the ball parallels this effortlessness in its gentle arc and its ultimate soft touch at the basket. The ball's reverse spin, imparted at release, is also counter to the forward motion of the ball. All elements are in perfect balance.

In Taoism, any phenomenal action or gesture manifests the two balanced cosmic forces of yin and yang. This is expressed powerfully by one of the world's greatest symbols of the fundamental polar nature of reality, a circle with a reverse S curve that divides the circle into two equal parts, one white and the other black, signifying any two opposites in the universe: day-night, positive-negative, male-female, active-passive, and so on. The black half contains a white dot and the white half contains a black dot signifying that nothing in the cosmos is purely yin or purely yang—each contains the seed of the other. Yang is positive, male, dry, hot, active, heavenly and strong. Yin is negative, feminine, damp, cold, dark, receptive, passive and earthly. The first words of Genesis also suggest this fundamental polarity underlying all things: "In the beginning, God created heaven and earth."

The outer circle of the yin-yang symbol represents the harmonious action of the Tao, since overall unity requires that oppositions apparent at a certain level be resolved in the total equilibrium of the whole. The total order of the cosmos results from the dynamic interplay of opposites. If one of the opposites disappeared, such as the negative charge on the electron, the universe as we know it would also disappear. When Neils Bohr, one of the giants of twentieth-century science, was knighted by the Danish Government, he chose the yin-yang symbol as his coat of arms. His research into the quantum world of the atom showed how the two poles of physical reality in apparent opposition collaborate harmoniously in the workings of the atomic universe.

The study of music gives us the most powerful model and symbol of inner harmony. Aesthetically, through our sense of "seeing," we perceive the convergence and divergence of reality as manifestations of beauty, order and their opposites. Yet only through our sense of hearing can we perceive the essence of the vibratory universe directly. In Hindu cosmology, sound is the first sensible quality produced out of the primordial ether. Since it is first in production, it has along with the sense of hearing a primary rank and infuses the other four senses of sight, touch, taste and smell.

The Pythagoreans saw the entire cosmos as organized on this principle of musical harmony. The heavenly spheres moved at distances directly proportional to the lengths of strings on a harp or lyre necessary to produce the notes of the musical scale. Only the initiates could hear the transcendent "music of the spheres" the heavenly bodies made as they moved through the imponderable ether. The more we find ourselves exclusively immersed in the secondary causes and effects described by modern science, the less we are tuned into this sense of harmony. Consequently, we lose the most refined form of higher cognition, a reflection of the original unity itself.

Harmony both reflects and reveals the profound mystery of the cosmos. This mystery touches the fathomless inwardness of the human being as it merges with the indefinite outwardness of the visible universe. Basic perception, an act of the intellect that allows the object to enter the subject, reveals this mysterious harmony and lies at the basis of all knowledge. Pure seeing without thought presents visible impressions to my retina and transfers these impressions to my brain in an impartial image that conveys both the unity and multiplicity of the cosmos.

I see the river, trees, birds, the passing boats, the sun's reflection on the water and the clouds in the distance in a single global image, all these separate elements in one sweeping unity. This immediate perception has a cosmic center that's inside me as well as in the external world. It contrasts sharply with what happens in conscious thought, where separate images file through my brain according to dictates of my ego, which divides subject from object, cutting me off from the universal harmony. Immediate perception dissolves the separation, revealing the underlying identity of seer and seen. "You are that," as the Vedanta, Taoism and Zen tell us.

Disharmony cannot exist in a positive sense in our thinking process: we can have only harmony or its absence. However, we can suffer disharmonious effects when we are unable to make accurate, logical distinctions that reflect true relations among phenomena, when we falsely identify impersonal events as functions of our egos, and when conflict and confusion dominate our awareness. We cannot find positive error in the intellect, just lack of truth. Either our intellect sees cosmic unity when ideas and forms come together around a center or it doesn't. Harmony, the dynamic balance of complementary poles, is a fundamental attribute of the universe; if we want to hear it, we must find ways to unblock our awareness. The act of listening from "deep and bottomless" emptiness joins us in the harmony of creation, freeing the mind from its conditioning.

The absence of a sense of harmony haunts our consciousness. We long for the equilibrium and stability that only harmony can provide. Intuitively, we know inner harmony leads to outer harmony and the person living in harmony lives in the unity of simplicity, seeing integration and wholeness at all levels of being. Soma and psyche are integrated in one whole, not divided against themselves. In the brain, the crowning faculty of reason and the subordinate faculties of imagination, emotion and sense work together as a magnificently sounding orchestra. The Taoists call the person who realizes this integration *chenn-jen*, or the true man.

Opposites must be in perfect equilibrium for harmony to exist in any of the manifested "ten thousand things." The jump shot expresses harmony through the dynamic interplay of weight and weightlessness, movement and stillness, great strength and effortlessness. The circle is closed with the complementarity of opposites.

The Sufi musician Hazrat Inayat Khan illuminated the spiritual nature of harmony:

Beauty is born of harmony. What is harmony? Harmony is right proportion, in other words right rhythm. And what is life? Life is the outcome of harmony. At the back of all creation is harmony, and the whole of creation is harmony. Intelligence longs to attain to the perfection of harmony. What man calls happiness is comfort, profit or gain, all he longs for and wishes to attain is harmony; in a smaller or greater degree he is longing for harmony.

16

Energy and Form

PERCEIVING THE UNIVERSE IS THE ACTION of seeing forms, colors and movement. This seeing gives us the impression that there are objects out there, so to speak, that are made of some solid substance commonly called matter. This concept of matter has been reinforced by classical physics since the seventeenth century. At that time, Descartes and Newton attempted to establish the philosophical foundation of a completely mechanical universe. Cosmic reality was reduced to solidity and motion, and measured by extension and time.

This reduction appeared necessary in order to measure physical reality. The flaws in this approach became apparent with advancing knowledge of relativity and quantum mechanics, where the subjective presence of human consciousness becomes integrally woven into the physical processes of nature. The classical idea of matter as an independent physical stuff with certain quantifiable characteristics vaporizes when we understand the universe as vibratory energy that includes the observer and human consciousness.

The apparently stable form an observer sees when looking at any object comes from the dynamic equilibrium of the object's oscillating atoms and molecules. According to physics, the perceived color results from the vibrating frequency of the electrons in response to the frequency of their illuminating light. The image formed in the mind is not, as is commonly thought, produced by the object: the vibrating panorama of form and color excites receptors in our sense organs that send signals for the brain to translate into a coherent image; therefore we can say the image pre-exists in the viewer. This means there is a latent structural identity between the object and the viewer—that is, a fundamental essence uniting the observer and the observed. As observers we don't perceive this identity because we assume an absolute separation between the world and ourselves, between subject and object. What is called satori, enlightenment or liberation is characterized by the liberating energy of total perception that removes the separation of subject and object.

Like perceptions of the outer world, inner perceptions are characterized by forms and vibratory states. The forms, images and ideas of consciousness are primarily a result of memory. They are positive or negative, depending on whether they affirm or deny our being. If the forms of memory are positive, our inner state reflects lightness and a sense of expansiveness. If the forms of memory are negative, our inner state is dark and contractive.

These basic movements of positive and negative states in the dreamlike condition of so-called waking consciousness represent energy lost in the endless debate between being and nothingness. The formless source of my being, called the Tao in Chinese philosophy, is free of these relative positive and negative states. Before it manifests in the world of matter, it is pure undifferentiated energy, beyond dualities.

YU: joy, enthusiasm

Physical gesture, as the ultimate expression of the inner person, is also a function of energy and form. The five-fold movement (crouch, stretch, lift, stroke and descent) of the jump shot, like any animate phenomenon, expresses inner and outer forms that are essentially energy. Its outer form is a dynamic conversion of mechanical energy, from potential (energy of position) to kinetic (energy of movement).

The external work—that is, the energy used to change the body's position—done on the athlete's center of mass starts at the lowest point of the crouch position. In the language of physics, this work equals the amount of force exerted on the floor by the shooter's muscles, multiplied by the distance the body's center of gravity moves. The overall work equals the change in potential energy of the athlete's center of gravity plus the kinetic energy the shooter has at liftoff. The athlete must maintain maximum force against the floor during the stretch segment since this provides explosiveness and directly results in good elevation or lift.

At the top of the jump, the velocity of the athlete is zero. Therefore, all the kinetic energy of the shooter's mass is now transformed into potential energy. Immediately before or at this point, the rotation and forward extension of the shooting arm does "work" on the ball; that is, it moves the ball through a maximum distance at full extension, imparting more energy to the ball as it leaves the finger tips. After release, the ball follows a parabolic curve as it arcs gracefully to the rim. During its trajectory, the ball possesses a combination of potential and kinetic energy in different amounts but the total energy always remains the same, as expressed by the law of conservation.

These multiple transformations of the mechanical energy of body and ball during the jump shot are driven by the production of organic energy in the body itself. Yet the question remains as to what initiates the production of this biochemical energy and what controls its coordination. Billions of cells from brain to muscle to limb are involved in this exceedingly complex process.

Energy itself is an elusive concept. We can easily identify its different forms—electrical, heat, nuclear, light and mechanical— and its transformations from one form to another. We can also see the effects of energy, which is the reason physicists define energy as the ability to do work. Nevertheless energy in itself is undefinable. Everything is ultimately energy, so nothing can contrast with it. In Hindu tradition, the god Shiva, as a dancer whose perpetual dance expresses the animate and inanimate cosmic movement, beautifully represents the continual flux of the dynamic patterns of energy changing into one another.

The invisible action of this Shiva-like motivating force, a direct flow from the formless source of one's being, is the ultimate coordinator of the biochemical, neurological, electrical and mechanical energy forms manifested in the jump shot gesture. The dance of the jump shot represents the play of this energy. As one commentator on the hexagram Yu from *The Book of Changes* or *I Ching* states: "The natural laws are not forces external to things, but represent the harmony of movement immanent in them."

17

Inner Blocking

PHYSICAL TALENT IS NO GUARANTEE OF consistently high quality performance. Strength, power and speed are often misspent if the psychological state of the athlete is unstable because of laziness, lack of clarity, indecisiveness, egoism or excessive emotionalism. These psychological problems are especially evident in shooting a basketball, since they become factors that act as inhibitors or blockages in executing the shooting gesture. These inner blockages are just as detrimental as the block of an opposing player.

The self-blocked shot is a powerful metaphor for the blockages of the birth of our inner energy. If we would allow ourselves to be inwardly attentive at our source, our inner state would be free of resistance; then our lives would have the possibility of flowing like the grace and beauty of the perfect jump shot. But too often we don't. We block ourselves just as a player, whose non-shooting hand rests on the ball, inhibits the shot's movement at release. The blockage of the inner flow of energy that lies at the basis of our psychological world creates a fundamental disturbance at the center of our lives. The ego sees this moving energy as a threat and resists it. Trapped in ignorance, the ego sees itself as immutable, the first cause of all things.

Though we may habitually try to, it's impossible to block this energy. We can only disintegrate it with image-making that ends up in a vicious circle of emotional rumination. This creates pain, suffering and confusion in the inner world.

A student once asked one of the Chinese masters for the most important word in Zen. The master replied, "Yes." This "yes," a total acceptance of what is (as opposed to hopeless resignation) is a return to the spontaneity, simplicity and innocence of childhood. It's what Jesus meant when he said, "Suffer little children and forbid them not, to come unto me: for of such is the kingdom of heaven." In other words, let the playful energy be unbound.

Our psychological world consists of the faculties of will, reason, imagination, emotion and memory. These work in conjunction with the five senses, three of which—seeing, hearing and touch—have primacy in athletics. Cooperation of all the faculties in a single harmonious unity is the antidote to the dispersion, agitation, conflict and disintegration we witness in athletics and other areas of life. Faculties working against themselves inhibit optimum performance.

Our faculties emanate from three fundamental centers: the intellectual center, the emotional center and the instinctive center. The intellectual center is located in the brain where the various cognitive acts such as induction, deduction and association co-exist with imagination. The emotional center lies in the upper torso, in the region of the heart. It is here that emotions, positive and negative, reflect our interactions with the outside world and our general sensibility to inner states. On this plane, our joys and sufferings play out their contrasting tones in response to the imaginative ruminations of a brain locked in a fictitious "I-centered" world. Our instinctive center is located at the base of the spinal column. As it does in non-human animals, this center expresses the physiological functions of sleep, sexual desire, hunger and thirst as well as the organic need to exist.

These centers, dynamic and interactive, continually affect each other. In cases of extreme egoism driven by pride, greed and excessive self-centeredness, the emotional center can experience violently contrasting highs and lows. A defeat or a case of misfortune can result in depression, which in turn can bring about a series of equally depressing images unrelated to the present circumstances. The instinctive center can be equally affected by these inner states, similarly expressing its disturbance by sleeplessness and a lack of appetite and sexual desire.

One can also try to isolate these centers from each other, for example, the intellectual center from the emotional center. The rationalist, under the false impression that reason is the sole guide for his actions, denies the fundamental role emotion plays. Only the liberated or enlightened human being has fully integrated all centers so they act as one. Then insight, an immediate perception that isn't emotional in character, allows total action, a completely appropriate response to the present situation. This insight is the root of compassion.

In actuality, dividing these centers is impossible. When reason tries to stifle emotion, the psychologist calls this repression. Its well-known effects can lead to extreme violence and chronic depression, common symptoms of modern life. In all cases where reason stifles the other faculties, rationalization—the tendency to justify rather than correct mistakes—prevails. This leads to unmitigated blindness, a self-centeredness that creates untold suffering for oneself and others. Conversely, emotion and instinct can suffocate reason and create similar forms of disorder. In athletics, particularly in shooting a basketball, these imbalances in the workings of the inner centers lead to inconsistency and erratic behavior both on and off the court.

Taoist tradition says a person unified with the Tao occupies "the invariable middle." This is the integral point where one's nature is concentrated, the place where all the human faculties and powers come together in a single dimensionless point. The Taoists refer to this point as the vital center of the human being and call it *hara*. It is from the hara that the swordsman or martial artist must act in order to master and perfect both craft and spiritual state.

In Hindu tradition, it is Brahma, the universal spirit, who dwells in this vital center. The "actionless activity" of this center governs behavior by the very fact that it doesn't participate in it. The Bhagavad Gita describes Krishna and Arjuna riding in the same chariot, a vehicle that symbolizes the human being. Arjuna fights the battle while Krishna steers. Simultaneously we have Krishna symbolizing the actionless activity of the immutable universal center and Arjuna symbolizing the relative action of the individual self.

The individual in most cases is totally unaware of the ultimate reality of the vital center's presence. This center is independent of the incessant agitation of the other three centers of emotion, thought and instinct. It is the immobility or stillness of these three centers that allows the powers of the soul to be integrated in the equilibrium of the unvarying middle, the central crossroads of our being.

The athlete whose thoughts, emotions and instincts are excessive, conflicting or unbalanced, blocks the free-flowing movement of skilled gesture. Consequently, the vital energy coagulates and impairs performance. As Chuang Tzu, the great Taoist sage who came immediately after Lao Tzu, stated: "Ears can only hear, mind can only think, but vital energy is empty, receptive to all things." When the vital energy acts as emptiness, the intelligence of pure, immediate response cuts through blockages. This action provides the shooter with calmness and pure vitality without the hindrance of emotion and distress.

18

Unconscious in the Zone

MOST OF US HAVE SOME EXPERIENCE of a transformation in which suddenly the familiar is bathed in an entirely new light. All the world loses its solidity. Things seem suspended in the golden light and our organism loses its substantiality, floating in the weightlessness of the eternal present. All is beauty, serenity and peace. Reality is not bathed in light but is light itself. The cosmos is, as the Koran tells us, a treasure of the hidden made manifest.

The ordinary transformed in the mysteries of the present is not unusual to the child, as Thomas Traherne, an eighteenth-century witness, tells us: "Is it not strange that an infant should be heir of the whole world, and see those mysteries which the books of the learned never unfold? The corn was orient and immortal wheat, which should never be reaped, nor was ever sown. I thought it has stood from everlasting to everlasting. The dust and stones of the street were as precious as gold: the gates were at the first end of the world. The green trees when I saw them first through one of the gates transported and ravished me, their sweetness and unusual beauty made my heart to leap, and almost mad with ecstasy, they were such strange and wonderful things. The men! O what venerable and reverend creatures did the aged seem! Immortal cherubim! And young men glittering and sparking angels, and maids strange seraphic pieces of life and beauty! Boys and girls tumbling in the streets and playing were moving jewels. I knew not that they were born or die; but all things abided eternally as they were in their proper places."

Our concepts of modern psychology offer little help in explaining such transformations. Freud and Jung would have us look below our surface consciousness to the unconscious to explain sudden changes of our inner states. According to Freud, what lies in the unconscious is unavailable to consciousness itself until it manifests its presence through dreams, inner conflicts, word associations and troubling behavior. The inner beast or id sits in the driver's seat of the unconscious, pushing the organism to satisfy unrestrained instinctual demands. Pleasure is its aim; it is totally heedless of any consequences resulting from its actions. The ego and superego, as Freud saw it, emerge from the id to negotiate, sublimate or control its incessant demands.

In contrast to Freud, Jung posited both a personal unconscious and a collective unconscious. The latter is like a dynamic memory bank of the entire human species accessible to each individual. Theoretically it contains archetypes not of transcendental principles but of myths, images, themes and patterns such as the solar hero, the mother-child relationship, and the flight from fear or danger. According to Jung, these underlie conscious acts and manifest themselves both in dreams and waking consciousness. They can function negatively when repressed or denied and not allowed full awareness by the conscious mind. These collective archetypes in Jung's theory can also act creatively and positively when accepted and integrated by the conscious ego.

In both theories, it would be better to call subconscious what is designated as unconscious, since there is no clear demarcation between the nature of consciousness and the make-up of the so-called unconscious. Consciousness and the subconscious are both individual and collective, rooted in the past, and contain mental forms as their content. All thoughts are images and propositions. Propositions are verbal or mathematical statements, and images are mental forms. Both move from the past to the future, obscuring awareness of the dimensionless present.

These descriptions are partially correct, but they are the tip of the iceberg. Outside and enveloping the deepest plane of consciousness, beyond the illusory debate between our being and nullity, lies the fundamental unconscious. No real separation exists between this unconscious and consciousness. Because we dwell exclusively in consciousness, the light and plenitude of the unconscious remain locked in the shadows. It is a mistake to associate the unconscious with the dark recesses and hidden satanic forces of the psyche. These are products of a repressed subconscious that self-knowledge has never illumined.

Jung himself spoke of this "transcendental psycho-physical background to our empirical world." Yet he remained locked in his theories of individuation and the collective unconscious. In these areas, he could never step outside of his dreams. But it is precisely this transcendental background—the "void" in Buddhist terminology—that opens a new dimension to human consciousness and provides the foundation of the transforming experience.

This void or fundamental unconscious represents absolute plenitude, since nothing exists outside of it. In Taoism, this void is called the infinite aspect of the Tao. Although veiled by incessant cerebral and emotional activity, which brings in its wake attachment to the forms of ordinary consciousness, this plenitude is the true spiritual heritage of every human being.

In a sport, the athlete whose performance transcends ordinary levels of excellence is "in the zone." The heightened awareness, the change in perception of space and time and the sense of absolute certainty, infallibility and rhythm in executing a physical gesture are all manifestations, however temporary, of the limitless possibilities of the unconscious. Here the athlete performs in the fullness of the immediate present, free of concept, executing his art to perfection. In one game of the National Basketball Association finals against Portland, Michael Jordan was shooting his jump shot with incredible accuracy, hitting six in a row from a three-point range. He just shrugged his shoulders while returning to the defensive end of the court as if to say, "I can't explain how this works."

Bobby Jones, one of the greatest golfers of all time, alluded to this phenomenon: "The golf swing is a most complicated combination of muscular actions, too complex to be controlled by objective conscious mental effort.... Consequently, we must rely a good deal upon the instinctive reactions acquired by long practice. It has been my experience that the more completely we can depend upon this instinct—the more thoroughly we can divest the subjective mind of conscious control—the more perfectly we can execute our shots."

For the athlete, the zone represents a rare and transitory phenomenon. Missing, of course, in this transitory eruption of the unconscious is the full and complete realization that infuses living with an infinite depth and expressionless meaning that can only be described as love—the total sensitivity and deep cosmic awareness of the order and perfection of all things.

19

Intensity and Inattention

ONE OF THE MOST PUZZLING ASPECTS in the execution of any artistic, scientific or athletic endeavor is inconsistency in performance. In athletics, this occurs individually and, at the team level, collectively. A pitcher has a no-hitter into the eighth inning and isn't fatigued. Suddenly, he begins to lose control and throws a pitch straight down the middle. The batter hits a home run, causing the pitcher to lose his no-hitter and his team to lose the game. A basketball team plays a near-perfect game in all areas—shooting, rebounding, steals, team assists, avoidance of turnovers, and defense—against a superior team, and in the next game falls apart against a mediocre team.

Some accept this breakdown at the individual and team level as the inevitable ebb and flow of human events. Others correctly see it as a purely mental problem. What exactly is this mental problem? Seeing skilled athletes miss layups, throw careless passes, react lethargically on defense and offense, allow opposing players uncontested shots, and shoot low percentage shots, one has to conclude it's a problem of inattention and lack of intensity.

This problem affects all areas of life, not just athletics. In business and daily life, inattention and mental lapses are responsible for billions of dollars in losses due to accidents, poor workmanship and inefficient service. On the personal level, it can result in human tragedies. In the home, the inattention of parents to their children results in physical and psychological suffering and wasted youth. The individuals who are the by-products of this neglect never realize full maturity. The costs of such inattention are incalculable.

The two words we stereotypically use as the cure for inattention are focus and concentration, which themselves are restrictions or fragmentations of consciousness that insulate us from our true center. If we tell someone to focus when he's shooting a foul shot, we are suggesting he form an image in his mind either of the shooting act or of the ball going through the rim. In some cases, the shooter can form both images sequentially. For some players, reciting a mantra is a form of focusing. To understand why this so-called focusing is actually inattention, we have to understand what is called total attention in Taoism and Zen.

Total attention is attention without object, or what Lao Tzu called being whole in the part. In other words, our awareness is in a state of total energy, joining subject and object in the essence that unites them beneath their apparent distinction. When the player looks at the basketball court, his immediate perception is of the floor, rim, backboard, ball, players, referees, scoreboard, clock, coaches and fans. The image formed in his awareness is a true replication or mirror image of this outer reality. Any observer would agree on the placement, color and shape of these objects.

This image is global, heterogeneous, unified and instantaneous. It is not a separate image such as exists in conscious
thought when the player grasps an aspect of the scene, such as
an opposing player or the rim, and begins to think about it. As
soon as the player selects an aspect of the scene, this process is
subject to time, since the image originates in a specific moment that has already passed. Thinking, which is a response of
memory—rooted in the past—fragments perception and oblit-
erates the timeless present. Only immediate perception allows
for total attention without concept.

Many people who suffer from mental disorders are exces-
sively focused on the images formed by their thinking process.
Frequently, they are so focused they can no longer give their
attention to what is going on around them, as is the case with
the obsessional neurotic. Concentration and focus imply selection and choice. Consequently the attentive powers of the mind
constrict. Athletics require a complete vision, one that allows a
competent response to a complex set of continually changing
circumstances. Only total attention can provide this response.

Once a great Zen master was asked by one of his students
to write some words of wisdom. The master wrote "attention."
The student then asked the meaning of attention. The master
then wrote, "Attention means attention." This may sound a little tautological, a needless repetition or circularity in reasoning
that leads nowhere. But this is exactly the point. Our immediate perception of the outer world, free of selectivity, choice, or
the machinery of thinking, is an act of pure intelligence.

As the mathematician and physicist Wolfgang Smith has recently commented, we have forgotten this direct intelligence
that "flies straight to the mark like an arrow; and much less do
we realize that this high and forgotten faculty—which the an-
cients termed 'intellect'—is operative and indeed plays the essential role in the act of sense perception." If the Zen master

had written any other definition than "Attention means attention," the student would have been lost in the snares of words and images. Total perception or total attention is indispensable in athletics and life. Our problems don't stem from a lack of focus but from the proverbial not seeing the forest for the trees.

Inattention creates a lack of intensity; the seeming intensity of excessive cerebration, which is diffused, wasted and restricted by images that constantly arise in the mind, is the product of restricted attention. How can a player be attentive to the demands of the moment if she's constantly occupied by the individual creations and psychological attachments of the mind?

Thinking as objective analysis has a proper and important role in skill mastery, practice and the preparation of game tactics and strategy. In the actual flow of the game, seeing immediately and responding correctly is a function of total attention for both players and coaches. This action is intensity itself and as the Taoist sage reminds us, "it is empty and formless," just as the Tao of heaven.

20

The Negative Way

GREAT HARM IS DONE TO HUMAN BEINGS by advisers who tell people facing difficult circumstances to "think positively" as a solution to life's difficulties. While thinking positively might provide some encouragement and emotional fortitude to the sufferer, it certainly doesn't solve anything in a fundamental and lasting way. Thinking positively as an emotional attitude or a form of self-will is significantly different from what is actually positive knowledge.

If a person is having some mechanical difficulties with a car that won't start, all the positive thinking in the world will not fix the problem, though it can encourage a person to keep trying, which does have some value. What will fix the problem is an understanding of the different components involved in the starting systems such as the battery, starter, relays, switch, plugs, distribution device, wiring, filters, injectors or carburetor, pump, and controls of the fuel-air systems. Also necessary is an understanding of how these components interact together. One must know what tests to do to identify the problem. This is the approach of positivism, an early twentieth-century philosophical movement that stresses what is knowable through logical reasoning, direct observation of the senses, and the experimental verifiability of tests. This detached approach of the positivistic method is a far cry from the emotionally based advice to "think positively."

Although positivistic approaches are a mode of formal knowledge, they contrast sharply with the esoteric doctrines of the Vedanta, Taoism, Chan and Zen. In these teachings, the Negative Way is the essential condition of ultimate truth and the solution to our existential dilemmas. Paradoxically, the Negative Way is not a "way" as the term is generally understood. The negatives of the Negative Way, such as emptiness, non-being and non-action, are not the opposites of positive statements; rather they indicate something wholly positive, something beyond any opposite.

Adherents to the Negative Way shun positive statements, considering them as limitations, fragments or shadows of reality. This is the reason the central tenets in Taoism and Chan always take a negative form—*wu-nien* or no thought, *wu-wei* or non-striving, no effort and non-action, and *wu-hsin* or no-mind (the fundamental unconscious). These are all Chinese negative expressions. The realization of *wu* or non-being became satori in Japanese Zen.

Advaita, another related word that comes from the Vedanta and has no equivalent in Western languages, roughly means non-duality. It expresses identification with the ultimate. Similarly, the English word infinite is a negative expression that means *not finite* but ultimately points to Nirvana, "the cessation of the turnings of the mind," reached through the extinction of craving, the "spiritual fasting" of Chuang-tzu.

A great Japanese sword master once described the effect of being without limits: "When I was twenty-four, I participated in a joint training session and engaged in one thousand four hundred matches over a seven-day period. I do not remember being tired or in pain. What is the secret? The mind has no limits." The inner infinite is the essential meaning of the negative tenets of Taoism, Chan and Zen and the doctrine of non-duality in the Vedanta. This meaning is the most affirmative of all conceptions because it is the absolute outside of which there is nothing.

Oscar Morganstern, who, along with the great mathematician John von Neumann, wrote *The Theory of Games and Economic Behavior*, says, "Some of the profoundest insights the human mind has achieved are best stated in negative form. . . . Though stated negatively, these and other discoveries are positive achievements and great contributions to human knowledge." In Chinese tradition, Confucianism teaches the positive way while Taoism provides the visionary precepts of the Negative Way.

The positive and negative ways have their place in the mastery of any art or technique. For mastery of the jump shot, practice needs to include both. The formal and informal can complement each other fully. The long solitary hours spent on some court where one can only hear the rhythmic bounce of the ball echoing into the vast silence are the perfect time to blend the negative way with the positive.

The shooter's awareness heightens as he senses the energy flowing through the body's systems up to the final release of the ball off the fingertips. A miss feels like a complete failure of brain and body, a breakdown of the energy of total attention. The analytic mind begins to seek the reasons. Did the wrist twist out of the vertical plane on release? Was the shot shortarmed by a premature release? Was the elbow aligned to the center of the rim? Was the ball resting only on the finger pad? Did the ball have proper backspin? Was there correct extension before release? Was the overall timing in both the vertical and horizontal plane correct? Was there proper containment or were too many muscle systems involved? Did the release feel effortless? Was the principle of the minimum force angle observed? Understanding the elements and synchronicity of the five-fold movement explained in Chapter Three allows one to identify the problem fairly quickly. This analysis is the positive way, but one must also give attention to the negative way.

The Fifth Happiness of Taoism reveals the negative way. The first four happinesses are longevity, posterity, great wisdom, and solitude. The Fifth Happiness isn't named because it's beyond the positive or relative good and therefore beyond words and distinctions. It is what Plotinus called "the flight of the alone to the alone." This requires abandoning the self, allowing one to fine tune the shot while deepening one's awareness of the absolute. The emptiness or void that envelops and penetrates every cell of our organism and everything in the universe is not to be feared. We welcome it as it embraces us in its infinity.

Negative attitudes have nothing to do with the Negative Way. These attitudes are reactions born of frustration and ignorance. A person who sees life through a psyche poisoned by cynicism, callousness, hate and self-preoccupation can't be in contact with the good, beautiful and true. An inversion that desensitizes the intelligence and cripples the emotions takes place psychologically. An athlete with a negative attitude has severely limited his possibilities. In team sports, the overall effect of this negative mental state is a contagious virus that debilitates team chemistry. In contrast, the Negative Way, which is always self-effacing in essence, allows an athlete to be fully engaged in all the positives, which include both personal excellence and team play.

21

Humility

OUR UNIVERSAL DIGNITY AS HUMAN BEINGS requires that we see our personal selves or egos as false centers that bring about unmitigated selfishness and distorted perceptions, which separate us from true humility or goodness, our fundamental nature. Lao Tzu tells us: "Those who are good I treat as good. But those who are not good, I also treat as good. For the original nature of man is goodness."

In a public arena such as athletics, where an athlete easily assumes a role as hero, the pretenses of the ego become inflated to vast proportions. The ego takes on the God-like and grandiose qualities associated with omnipotence. This ultimate self-centeredness denies our true center, the spirit of team play and total commitment to skill mastery.

It's no wonder that NBA and college statistics reveal a waning of skill level. Free-throw and field-goal percentages are lower in 1998 than they were twenty years ago. Commentators and analysts acknowledge these falling numbers with their critical observations on the game. Discipline (the root of the word means "to learn") and the commitment necessary for technical mastery come easily when the pretensions of the ego are absent. Oscar Robertson, one of the greatest players to ever play the game, recently commented on this lack of commitment and discipline in players who "see themselves as entities greater than the game, and selfishness rules. . . . This thinking carries over into their irresponsible lifestyles."

Unfortunately, this inflated self-indulgence results in more than a lack of skill mastery. Self-centeredness extends itself in anti-social acts that convey disrespect for universal civilized norms, authority and team structure. Some fans sympathize with these anti-social and irresponsible acts, providing a convoluted rationale seasoned with emotionally charged language.

Even in the most intimate human relationships, egocentricity rears its ugly head. Krishnamurti, in describing the spread of self-centeredness, states: "It also expresses itself in the family; the father pursues his own selfishness in all ways of his life and so does the mother. Fame, good looks form a basis of this hidden, creeping movement of the self." One sees the sad effects of this movement in all areas of life.

What is the root cause of this unmitigated selfishness? Does the answer lie in a culture and society that champion freedom bordering on license — an abdication of responsibility? Is it because our society treasures personal opinion above the universal perception of truth? Is it because we encourage indulgence in the pleasures of consumerism, animal appetite, and easy stimulation of the senses? Is it because our society neglects the refined sensibilities that would grow easily and steadily in a climate of self-denial? Is it the inevitable consequence of a secular world that denies human links to the divine?

This collective deterioration certainly reflects disorder at the individual level. We are reminded here of the biblical injunction: "By their fruits ye shall know them." Our nature as human beings is to reflect divine attributes and be aware of the flaws of the human state. One of the most basic of these flaws is our tendency to view ourselves as self-contained and self-sufficient entities cut off from a transcendent reality. Meister Eckhart reminded us that "the restlessness of all our storms comes from self-will whether we know it or not." Some modern athletes, with their bloated contracts, represent this perversity to an extreme degree. They show little or no magnanimity, a sense that they would like to make the world a better place. We can see the effects of such attitudes both on and off the court.

This personal narcissism causes a collective narcissism that creates havoc in daily life, in the world as a whole and in team sports. It begins in the early stages of life and gathers momentum throughout life. The great esoteric traditions see narcissism, this inordinate sense of self, as the basic human failing, the cause of much suffering and conflict.

What will eliminate this self-love based on the illusory division of "self" and "not-self"? This obsession denies the transforming power of reality that occurs when one sees how the outside world is inseparable from the self. Plato referred to all perceptions and actions of the divided self as the "shadows of the cave." These shadows point to the gnawing emptiness, loneliness and lack of meaning in the human condition when we lose contact with the source of all things.

The teachings of Taoism and Zen address the problems of the I-centered human condition by directly pointing to the mind's essence, as described in a short verse from the Tang Dynasty:

A special transmission outside scriptures;

No dependence upon words and letters;

Direct pointing to the mind;

Seeing into one's own nature and realizing Buddhahood.

When asked by an emperor of the same dynasty to explain how the fundamental principles of Zen relate to meditation tech-

niques, Huineng, the most influential of the Chinese Zen Patri-
archs, expressed the doctrine of awakening to the eternal state
through direct insight: "The truth is understood by the mind
and not by sitting in meditation. To see that all things are empty
is to practice sitting in meditation. Ultimately there is neither
attainment nor realization; how much less sitting in meditation
. . . let the mind move on as it is in itself and perform its inexhaustible functions. This is the way to be in accord with the
mind-essence." Even techniques intended to free us can seduce
and trap us into believing we're important, thereby negating the
root purpose of the techniques. Insight can arrive by many
means, but grasping or clinging to a method pushes it away.

The fictitious "I" or "self" can only be defined by saying what
it is not. It is not my body nor my mind nor anything else in the
universe. As a formless, insubstantial entity, this "I" assumes the
role of a central processing unit, a controller of one's organism,
a miniature first cause within a personalized universe. It forms
the basis of prevailing and misconstrued ideas of individualism.

The absolute zero of the "I" is humility, the mystical surrender of self. Meister Eckhart describes this ultimate detachment
as an interior journey to the absolute good. He states, "If I were
up here, and I said to someone, 'Come up here,' that would be
difficult. But if I were to say, 'Sit down there,' that would be
easy. God acts like that. If a person humbles himself, God cannot withhold his own goodness but must come down and flow
into the humble person, and to him who is least of all he gives
himself the most of all, and he gives himself to him completely.
What God gives is his being, and his being is his goodness, and
his goodness is his love."

The athlete who can see through the false division set up by
the thinking process and its false metaphysical assumptions is
free from the disorder, contradictions and psychological rigidity

of the self. Humility, surrender of the self, brings about an awareness that functions in the timelessness of the present. The athlete then easily and naturally devotes total energy to skill mastery and team play. For there is no "I" in awareness or in team play.

22

The Coach as "True Man"

THE CONCEPTION OF WHAT A HUMAN BEING IS and the possibilities of human development have narrowed considerably during the last four hundred years. The modern human being is now seen through the distorted lenses of humanism and evolutionism. Humanism projects the person as a self-sufficient whole with reason as our highest faculty. Evolution sees us as byproducts of millions of years of the random forces of natural selection, which finally place us at the summit of the animal kingdom. These twin pillars of modern thought can be considered a philosophical outgrowth of the success the theories of Newtonian mechanics had in describing the natural world.

For the followers of Newton (nearly all of modern humanity) reason is restricted to the guidelines of practical experiment and measured quantities. As a result, the radiant intellect that opens humanity to the vistas of the absolute and places us above the angels in the fabric of creation becomes, in the derivative materialistic philosophies, only a word without its original significance. Having arrived at this point, we can draw only one conclusion: without intellect, the human being is just another member of the animal kingdom.

Leonardo da Vinci symbolically represented the possibilities of the infinite faculty of human intellect. He combined two figures drawn by the Roman architect Vitruvius, who had studied the proportions of the human being as a model to be used in buildings. Da Vinci synthesized the drawings by placing a man in two different positions within a circle and a slightly overlapping square. The bottom side of the square is tangent to the circle and the top side cuts the circle approximately two thirds of the radius up from the center. The man's navel is at the center of the circle. His horizontally outstretched arms and legs drawn together form one figure where the fingertips touch the vertical sides of the square and the soles of the feet touch the bottom side. Here the human figure reveals the proportions of a perfect square, the geometric form symbolizing the earth or manifestation. The second human figure superimposed over the first is depicted with arms raised at a slight angle from the horizontal and legs spread outward. The fingertips and soles of the feet now touch the circumference of the circle, and here the human form yields a perfect circle, the form that symbolizes the action of the divine.

The understanding that a human being, besides synthesizing all the elements of nature, is the great symbol of the mystery of the divine in the universe is lost to the modern world. One of the ways Taoism expresses this great depth and mystery is in the very ideograph of the Tao. It combines the signs for the head and the feet, thereby implying that the human is the true measure of all things physical and spiritual.

If a coach, oblivious to this mystery, sees players only by the functions they perform on the court or field, he misses the most important dimension. Such a coach's ambition for success often blinds him to the need for in-depth understanding and compassion in his relationship with players. Some coaches, who have been blessed with talent, may have successful records. Nevertheless, they still don't have what the Taoists call *te*, uprightness or virtue. If a coach possessed this non-cultivated virtue, his players would feel they were coached by someone whose understanding transcends X's and O's.

The action of the Tao is *te*; te words appear together in the title Tao Te Ching. *Te* is not a social or human moral ideal but the spontaneous unfolding of the perfection of the Tao. A coach infused by *te* would be like Plato's philosopher-king, a leader whose spiritual depth provides the magnetic cohesiveness that brings out the best in the players, sport and life. *Te* is sometimes translated as virtue. This virtue is not the result of training oneself to face circumstances in the light of social respectability. *Te* always lies beyond ordinary social conventions and conditioned responses.

When we observe team play, we consider it the result of good chemistry, but unity would be a better word. Unity starts with the coach, who must be a master of the technical aspects of the sport. And it is the coach who must provide the point of balance for the team, through the action of uprightness or *te*. Here an invisible center of gravity gives a spiritual equilibrium to the team.

In Taoism, this is the function of the "True Man," who has inwardly returned to his nonformal center, or what is called "the heart." This heart is not the physical organ but "the invariable middle" that is free from all the viscitudes of existence, including winning and losing. In the language of Western Hermeticism, the heart is the gateway to the self-revelation of the absolute. This is an androgynous state in which all the powers of being are unified, all opposites are balanced, the male and female aspects of the psyche are in harmony.

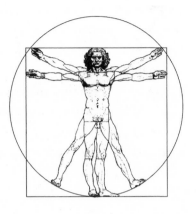

Today's coaches, for the most part, exhibit little of this balance. In many cases, they exhibit considerable disturbances of a psychological nature. Obviously many have not considered the importance of unifying their inner nature through self-understanding and a self-effacing humility. The manifestations of egoism are apparent in their behavior, in their approach to their team and to the game in general. *Te*, the pillar of uprightness, is missing.

The absence of this vertical dimension, which includes what John Wooden calls "the great certitude," distorts the horizontal dimension, the technical knowledge of the game. Fear of losing, for instance, causes some coaches to institute game strategies and styles of play directly antithetical to the spirit and fundamental nature of the game. Excessive aggressiveness and a slowed tempo inhibit the possibilities of the game. Listen to the late astronomer Carl Sagan extol the virtues of basketball: "This is fundamentally not a contact sport like football. It's a game of finesse . . . a coordination of intellect and athleticism, a harmony of mind and body. . . . Basketball has become—at its best—the paramount synthesis in sport of intelligence, precision, courage, audacity, anticipation, artifice, teamwork, elegance and grace." A coach whose perspective is limited to one dimension will not inspire this kind of love and appreciation of the game nor will he help his players have right values and place all things relative and absolute in perspective.

The outward and inward dimensions are always present with the coach who represents "true man." *Te*, uprightness—with its attending virtues of order, beauty, goodness and fairness—

becomes a vibration that invigorates and harmonizes the team. This "actionless action" plays the true pivot around which all things turn in perfect equilibrium. Chuang Tzu says this of the true man: "Occupying a man's body, he is no longer a man. . . . What makes him still a man is something infinitely small. What makes him one with heaven is infinitely large." The coach as "true man" will respond in a gracefully competent manner to all circumstances and challenges as they arise.

23

Shooting as Art

IN TAOISM, THE ART OF THE DIVINE is always one of transformation. The state of mind touching this transforming movement always reflects an unpremeditated, non-mediated relationship with nature; this is paramount in the execution of any art. In an art such as landscape painting, the artist depicts the movement of nature against a hidden or ineffable still center, capturing both the transient, dynamic aspect and the complementary static aspect. In this way, space (as simultaneity) is united to time (as movement) in what the physics of relativity calls the space-time continuum.

It is not only the universe of space-time that Taoist art or sacred art in general reveals, but what Aristotle called the "unmoved mover," the perfect void behind all the moving phenomena of existence, where opposites are reconciled. This void in itself is immovable; yet it is simultaneously the "cosmic bellows" of Lao Tzu, inexhaustible in its creative activity. The great

 symbol of Taoist art is a disc with a hole in the center: the solid part of the disc represents the universe and the void in the middle symbolizes the inherent and transcendent center.

By uniting the static and dynamic aspects of reality and defining a perfect equilibrium between the vertical and horizontal, the jump shot expresses this art of transformation. The shooter of the jump shot, a divine animal with vertical gait and posture, ascends into space with upward aspiration. This movement ends in a perfect stasis. It is this momentary pause at the top of the ascent that allows the spherical ball, the symbol of undifferentiated unity, to find the center of the rim, symbol of the ineffable and immutable source of all things. This immobilization and tension at the top of the jump synthesizes the active and the passive. In principle this is no different from the archer's stance at the moment of release or the Taoist artist's tense pause before executing a brush stroke. Movement out of stillness gives birth to the new.

At the heart of this gesture-art is a profound symbolism. The athlete ascends from the court, a four-sided rectangular shape symbolic of the earth. The number four is always associated with such aspects of the earth as the four fundamental forces (gravity, electromagnetism, the strong nuclear force and the weak nuclear force), the four classifications of matter (elements, compounds, solutions and mixtures), the four cardinal points and the four seasons.

The circularity of the rim and the parabolic flight-curve of the ball complement the rectangularity of the court. All curves, and the circle in particular, are celestial. The uprightness of the body and its vertical ascent are symbolic of the unique place the human holds in the cosmos as mediator between earth and heaven. The distance the ball traverses horizontally balances the vertical. Considering all these factors, it isn't surprising that the game of basketball was invented in the Young Men's Christian Association by a seminary student who became a doctor. Its spiritual roots are evident.

Most athletes are unaware of the spiritual and artistic dimensions of skilled gesture. Fans pour into arenas thirsting to see sport raised to heroic heights only to frequently witness mediocrity in different forms. Unfortunately these fans see athletes who often substitute emotional outbursts for real skill and team play, demonstrating their fever and restlessness, which indicate a lack of inner equilibrium. The athlete who seeks to combine the spiritual resources of his being with the artistry and athleticism of the game must be as self-effacing as the Taoist artist is before the wonders and mysteries of nature. The soul can only be in harmony when the endless tensions and irrational impulses to satisfy desires cease. Only then can the player regain the lost connection to possibilities of inward depth. As Shakespeare says:

Such harmony is in immortal souls.
But whilst this muddy vesture of decay
Doth grossly close it in we cannot hear.

Practice affords the athlete the opportunity to perfect her craft and reflect on the higher meaning of her calling. Here a distinction needs to be made between habit and routine. Habit is a mental repetition, thoughts repeating the same patterns in the brain day in and day out. The brain cells become crippled and begin to decay, causing an ultimate shrinkage in brain size. How extraordinary this is! The three-pound hemispherical brain, suggesting the heavenly dome of sacred art and architecture, is the most complex object in the universe. Its two hundred billion neurons and trillion supporting cells have more connections than the number of stars in the universe. Habit calls into action a miniscule portion of these circuits and leads ultimately to brain shrinkage and deterioration.

What does this say about the repetitive practice required for skill mastery? The answer to this lies in an understanding of time. Imposing memory on the stream of existence creates time—we return to the past in our memories as we travel through the unfolding present to the future. In this way, we carry the past with us so it too moves through the present to the future. Our divisions of time, such as the second, minute and hour, are measurements that refer to a movement in space: the hands of a clock, the earth's movement around the sun. So time in this sense is a measure of motion.

The present is the connecting link between yesterday and tomorrow, before and after, past and future. The moving present is different from the non-moving moment, which has no duration and is totally indivisible. The moment is the eternal now—the experience of total, immediate attention—and is the immutable fabric from which all moving time is made. It is not in time, so it reflects the tranquil equilibrium and static perfection of the center.

Any skilled performer who sees the craft, skill or art as an expression of a fundamental spiritual dimension always practices and performs *sub specie aeternatatis*, under the domain of the eternal now. In ancient Roman civilization, the Guild of Artisans presided over the solstice feasts of Janus—the god of gates and doorways, a symbolic divine being with two human faces looking in opposite directions—on the first day of summer and winter. The opposed faces of Janus look to the past and the future, but the present or eternal moment is represented by the face that isn't there, since the eternal cannot be drawn or measured on the face of time. The true artist always works from this invisible yet intuitively obvious dimension.

True practice or performance is not a dulling habit repeated over and over again. In practicing the jump shot, one works continuously on the qualitative perfection and consistency of form just as a classical pianist or dancer does. However, the athlete as artist realizes that yesterday is not today. His energy and attention are free of the thought forms that create the divisions of time. This attention is total in the dimensionless present. Each shot is renewed, not repeated. As Hubert Benoit says of the universal mind that participates in the timelessness of the moment, "Without duration, but always renewing, it is discontinuous by its instantaneousness and continuous by its constant renewal: as evanescent as the instant, it participates in eternity."

Without the burdens of inattention, laziness and pride, the pure shooter can then realize, in the stillness of the moment, a pure creation in the perfect line of gesture, rhythmically harmonious in body and spirit and therefore in keeping with all great art.

BIBLIOGRAPHY

Hubert Benoit, *Let Go*. Trans. Albert W. Low (New York: George Allen and Unwin, 1962).

Hubert Benoit, *The Supreme Doctrine*, (New York: The Viking Press, 1967).

Peter Brancasio, *Sport Science: Physical Laws On Optimum Performance* (New York: Simon and Schuster, 1984).

Titus Burckhardt, *Mirror of the Intellect* (Albany: State University of New York Press, 1987).

Sophia Delza, *The Tai Chi Chuan Experience* (Albany: State University of New York Press, 1966).

Gia-Fu-Feng and Jane English, *Chuang Tzu* (New York: Alfred A. Knopf, 1974).

Rene Guenon, *The Reign of Quantity and the Sign of the Times*, trans. Lord Northbourne (London: Luzac & Company, 1953).

Eugen Herrigal, *Zen In The Art of Archery*, trans. R.F.C. Hiel (New York: Vantage Books, 1971).

Toshihiko Izutsi, *Sufism and Taoism* (Berkeley: University of California Press, 1988)

J. Krishnamurti, *The First and Last Freedom* (New York: Harper and Row Publishers, 1954).

Lao Tzu, *Tao Te Ching*, trans. James Legge (New York: Dover Publications, 1962).

Joscelyn Godwin, in *Music Mysticism and Magic* (New York: Routledge and Kegan Paul, 1986)

George Kovacs, *Zen Hoops: The Spiritual Beauty of Basketball* (Lewiston, New York: The Edwin Mellen Press, Ltd., 1993).

Oscar Robertson, "Instead of Hoops, the Blame Game," *The New York Times* 7 Nov. 1998.

Oscar Morganstern, "Limits of the Uses of Mathematics in Economics" in *Symposium on Mathematics and the Social Sciences*, June 1963, by The American Academy of Political an Social Sciences; quoted by Benjamin Bold in *Famous Problems of Geometry* (New York: Dover Publications Inc., 1982).

Frithjof Schuon, *In the Face of the Absolute* (Bloomington, Indiana: World Wisdom Books, Inc., 1989).

Wolfgang Smith, *The Quantum Enigma* (Peru, Illinois: Sherwood Sugden & Company, 1995).

John Stevens, *The Sword of No Sword* (New York: Shambhala, 1984).

Thomas Traherne, *Centuries of Meditation* (London: Dobel, 1948).

R. Wilhelm, *The I Ching or Book of Changes* (Princeton: Princeton University Press, 1967).

Other Seastone Titles

MUSIC OF SILENCE
David Steindl-Rast with Sharon Lebell   Introduction by Kathleen Norris
A noted Benedictine monk shows us how to incorporate the sacred meaning of monastic life into our everyday world by paying attention to the "seasons of the day" and the enlivening messages to be found in each moment. *Trade paper. $12.00*

BEFORE HE WAS BUDDHA: THE LIFE OF SIDDHARTHA
Hammalawa Saddhatissa   Introduction by Jack Kornfield
Written in a lucid, flowing style, this biographical profile reveals the strength and gentleness of Buddha's character and brings to life the compassion that gave his teachings universal appeal. *Hardcover. $16.00*

JESUS AND BUDDHA: THE PARALLEL SAYINGS
Marcus Borg, Editor   Introduction by Jack Kornfield
Traces the life stories and beliefs of Jesus and Buddha, then presents a comprehensive collection of their remarkably similar teachings on facing pages. *Hardcover. $19.95*

A.D. 1000: A WORLD ON THE BRINK OF APOCALYPSE
Richard Erdoes   Introduction by Karen Armstrong
A chilling account of a chaotic time with unnerving parallels to our own, this book brings us the life and career of Pope Sylvester II, a visionary so brilliant many of his contemporaries assumed he had made a pact with the devil. *Trade paper. $14.95*

UNEARTHING THE LOST WORDS OF JESUS:
THE DISCOVERY AND TEXT OF THE GOSPEL OF THOMAS
John Dart and Ray Riegert   Commentary by John Dominic Crossan
Details the discovery of the greatest collection of apocryphal Christian documents ever found. The dramatic narrative history is combined with an annotated translation of The Gospel of Thomas. *Hardcover. $17.00*

AMERICAN INDIAN GENESIS: THE STORY OF CREATION
Percy Bullchild   Introduction by Mary Crow Dog
Written as it has been spoken for generations in the Blackfeet style, this provocative work provides a Plains Indian history of the world's creation. *Hardcover. $17.00*

THE PSALMS IN HAIKU: MEDITATIVE SONGS OF PRAYER
Father Richard Gwyn

Here are praises to spiritual power presented in a stark and clear fashion, in the ancient Japanese form of haiku poetry. These vivid and deeply moving versions will challenge those familiar with the Psalms to look for new meaning while introducing the prayers to a whole new audience. *Trade paper. $14.00*

DAVID: POWER, LUST AND BETRAYAL IN BIBLICAL TIMES
Jerry M. Landay

The personal story of a man of ambition, complexity, talent and human frailty, one of the most popular heroes of the ancient world is portrayed here with the care of a historian and the color of a novelist. *Hardcover. $19.00*

JESUS THE MAGICIAN: CHARLATAN OR SON OF GOD?
Morton Smith   Introduction by Russell Shorto

Challenging the accepted Christian image, *Jesus the Magician* introduces us to a complex and enigmatic man whose contemporaries perceived him as a magician, even a trickster. Smith relies both on the Gospels and on what was said of Jesus by those who did not believe in him. *Trade paper. $13.95*

APOCALYPSE 2000: THE BOOK OF REVELATION
John Miller, Editor   Introduction by Andrei Codrescu

Apocalypse 2000 brings the fascinating Book of Revelation to life with rich illustrations and modern reflections about the apocalypse by notable contemporaries. *Hardcover. $17.95*

DEAD SEA SCROLLS: THE COMPLETE STORY
Dr. Jonathan Campbell

Dispels rumors surrounding the Scrolls and recounts the actual events of their unearthing, laying the groundwork for a vivid investigation of the relevance of the Scrolls to our times. *Trade paper. $12.95*

To order these titles or other Seastone books call 800-377-2542 or 510-601-8301, e-mail ulysses@ulyssespress.com or write to Ulysses Press, P.O. Box 3440, Berkeley, CA 94703. There is no charge for shipping on retail orders. California residents must include sales tax. Allow two to three weeks for delivery.

JOHN F. MAHONEY is a basketball coach and has translated several books on psychology and religion, including *The Interior Realization* and *Nirvana Tao*. He lives in Newark, New Jersey.

BILL WALTON, currently a sports commentator for NBC, is a member of the National Basketball Association Hall of Fame. As a professional basketball player he was an All-Star with the Portland Trailblazers.